ROCK

DEVOTIONAL

100 DAYS
TO KNOW AND TRUST
GOD'S TRUTH

written by Rhonda VanCleave

B&H
kids
Brentwood TN

INTRODUCTION

The truth in God's Word is rock solid!

Voices of culture are strong and pervasive. As a kid, you are surrounded by half-truths or even full lies about God and people. The world's meaning of the word "truth" is constantly changing; that's why it's so important to know where you can find *God's* truth. It has never changed, and it never will. The truth in God's Word stands strong like a towering rock—a beacon calling all people to hold tight to it so that we don't get tossed about by each new crashing wave.

Over the next one hundred days, you will encounter several modern lies disguised as truths you may have heard before. Through daily Bible verses, stories, prayer prompts, and activities, you will find that the Bible contains rock-solid truth. You can learn to rely on God's truth to better trust and follow Him. Sometimes, the truth in God's Word will seem radically different from what the rest of the world tells you. God does not want you just to go along with what the world says; He wants you to set your mind on God's truth so you can follow Him.

Do not be conformed to this age, but
be transformed by the renewing of
your mind . . .—Romans 12:2

1

Whoever speaks the truth declares what is right, but a false witness speaks deceit.
—Proverbs 12:17

Ｈow do you know when someone is telling the truth?" Colter asked his mom.

Mom thought for a minute. "That can be hard to know, Colt," she answered. "First, I consider who it is. Can I trust that person? Is he or she typically a reliable source? Think about this. Do you remember when Mr. Johnson told you hummingbirds can fly backward? Why did you believe him?"

"Mr. Johnson has tons of hummingbird feeders," answered Colter. "He even belongs to a group that studies hummingbirds. Oh, I see what you mean. I can trust Mr. Johnson to know about hummingbirds because he's a reliable source."

Colter knew he could trust Mr. Johnson to know the truth about hummingbirds. More importantly, our Bible is a reliable source for many things we need to know.

As you read the devotions in this book, you'll learn more about why you can trust what the Bible tells you and discover some of the truths in the Bible.

KITE WORDS

What words do you think of when you think about TRUTH?
Write words that describe "truth" on the kite tail.

***Thank God for giving us
His words in the Bible.***

2

Be diligent to present yourself to God as one approved, a worker who doesn't need to be ashamed, correctly teaching the word of truth.—2 Timothy 2:15

You may know some people who read the Bible a lot and talk about what the Bible says. They probably think the Bible is the most valuable thing ever. You may know other people who think the Bible is an old book that doesn't apply to anyone's life anymore. What is the truth?

Did you know the Bible has sixty-six books that were written by several authors over the course of hundreds of years? The Bible as we know it was put together about two thousand years ago. So, yes, it is an old book. But it is called "God's Word" because, even though people wrote the words a long time ago, God is in control of everything in the Bible. He spoke to the people who wrote in the Bible; it's God's message written down by human beings. And His words are for us today too!

Did you know that people who study the Bible discover more things as they spend time reading it? God helps us understand what we read. Sometimes our parents or Bible teachers help us learn more about what the Bible says too. But, most importantly, God's Spirit teaches us. The Spirit helps us to learn about God as we study His Word.

SCRIBBLES IN THE SAND

On the sand below, write the names of people who help you know more about the Bible. Pray for them.

As you pray and read your Bible, ask God to help you understand and know His truth.

3

Now Ezra had determined in his heart to study the law of the Lord, obey it, and teach its statutes and ordinances in Israel.—Ezra 7:10

Ezra was someone who lived during Old Testament times in Babylon, far away from his home country. Most of the people where Ezra lived did not worship the one true God, but Ezra was determined to learn about God and study God's Word. At that time, only part of the Bible had been written.

Eventually, Ezra was allowed to travel all the way back to a city called Jerusalem in his home country. Many Jewish people joined Ezra in the move back to Jerusalem. Ezra was sad when he arrived. So many of his people had stopped reading and studying God's Word. Ezra shared his sadness with the people, and God used Ezra to help the people begin to learn from God's Word and obey God again.

Do you think it was hard for Ezra to encourage others to study God's Word? Do you have people who encourage you to read and study God's Word?

BONFIRE PRAYERS

Write a prayer to God in the bonfire below. Ask Him to help you study His Word (the Bible).

Ask God to help you want to study your Bible.

4

The entirety of your word is truth, each of
your righteous judgments endures forever.
—Psalm 119:160

Isabella sat down on the couch and began turning pages in her Bible. "I know I'm supposed to read my Bible, but there are lots of pages, and I don't know where to start."

Abuela looked up from her sewing and smiled. "Do you remember that great big turkey we had for Thanksgiving?"

"It was huge!" Isabella exclaimed. "It was the best turkey you've ever cooked!"

"Did you pick up the whole thing and eat it right then?" Abuela asked.

"No," Isabella laughed, shaking her head. "You let me have my favorite part. Then I went back for more. I remember we had lots of great meals all week from that turkey."

Abuela nodded. "That's right. Reading your Bible is the same. Start with something you enjoy and keep going. You might pick one of the Gospels, like Luke, and begin there. The important thing is to keep reading and rereading. God always has things to show you—even in the parts you might not expect to love."

BEACHCOMBING FINDS

Locate Psalm 119 in your Bible. Read each of the verses listed on the shells and write something that the verse says about God's Word on that shell.

Psalm 119:11

Psalm 119:16

Psalm 119:34

Psalm 119:97

Psalm 119:44

Psalm 119:105

Tell God you want to read your Bible every day.
Ask Him to help you.

5

All Scripture is inspired by God and is profitable for teaching, for rebuking, for correcting, for training in righteousness, so that the man of God may be complete, equipped for every good work.—2 Timothy 3:16–17

Today's verse has a lot to say about what the Bible does: teaching, rebuking, correcting, and training in righteousness. What does all that mean, and how does God's Word (Scripture) do that?

God's Word *teaches* us the truths we need to know. Truth is not just what someone thinks, but what God says is true.

God's Word *rebukes*, which means it helps point out things that are wrong. Sometimes the things we hear or read in the world may sound right, but the Bible helps us know the difference between a person's opinion and God's truth.

God's Word *corrects* us. Just like the adults in our lives who correct our wrong behavior, God's Word helps us know the things that dishonor Him.

God's Word *trains us in righteousness*. Righteousness means living in the right way. God's Word also helps us know how to do the right things by obeying God and honoring God.

God's Word is a wonderful gift from God. It teaches us and guides us, but most of all, it helps us know about the God who loves us.

SEASIDE FUN

Can you find these words from 2 Timothy 3:16–17 in the word search? Do you remember what they mean?

Word Bank: TEACHING CORRECTING REBUKING
TRAINING INSPIRED SCRIPTURE EQUIPPED

K	G	T	E	B	N	T	C	G	G
I	A	G	Q	M	Y	R	O	T	S
N	T	Z	P	E	T	E	R	L	C
S	R	H	M	Q	E	B	R	W	R
P	A	C	M	U	A	U	E	W	I
I	I	M	V	I	C	K	C	X	P
R	N	J	I	P	H	I	T	Q	T
E	I	X	G	P	I	N	I	W	U
D	N	L	Q	E	N	G	N	E	R
M	G	R	P	D	G	R	G	Q	E

Thank God for the many ways His Word helps us grow into people who honor and please Him.

6

*No prophecy ever came by the will of man;
instead, men spoke from God as they were
carried along by the Holy Spirit.—2 Peter 1:21*

Jesse listened carefully while his Bible study teacher explained how the Bible was divided into two sections called "Testaments." The Old Testament described events before Jesus's lifetime. The New Testament described events surrounding Jesus's birth, ministry, death, and resurrection. It also described the times of the early church. When the teacher said there were sixty-six books in the Bible with many different writers, Jesse's hand flew into the air. "What is it, Jesse?" his teacher asked.

"I thought the Bible is God's Word," Jesse said. "How can it be God's Word if people wrote it?"

"Great question," his teacher replied. Then she read 2 Peter 1:21 to the group. "You see," she explained, "God the Holy Spirit guided their writing so that it wasn't their 'will' or what they thought that made them write the words of the Bible. The words were God's message. God has been in control of His Word through the centuries so that His message is clear. It has always been the same, and it has always been God's words."

KITE WORDS

What words do you think of when you think about the Bible?
Write words on the kite tail that describe what you think of
when you think about the Bible.

Thank God for the way He guided people
to write down His messages.

7

This is why we constantly thank God, because when you received the word of God that you heard from us, you welcomed it not as a human message, but as it truly is, the word of God.—1 Thessalonians 2:13

Emma heard Nana's phone make a little chirping noise. "Is that another text from Grandpa?" Emma asked.

"Yes," Nana said as she smiled. "He sent me a picture of the fish he just caught."

"Did Grandpa text you like that when you were dating?" Emma giggled.

"Oh my, no!" Nana laughed. "We didn't even have cell phones then. Sometimes, when I was away at college, we just wrote letters. Those were special messages. I still have them. But do you know what message is even more special to me than Grandpa's letters?"

"No! What could be more special than that?" Emma exclaimed.

Nana held up the Bible she had been reading. "God's Word is a very special message because it's not just from a human being. It's from God Himself," Nana explained. "These are the most special messages of all!"

SCRIBBLES IN THE SAND

What are some messages, or truths, you have already learned from God's Word? Scribble them in the sand.

Thank God for His messages in the Bible that help you know how much He loves you.

8

But the wisdom from above is first pure, then peace-loving, gentle, compliant, full of mercy and good fruits, unwavering, without pretense.—James 3:17

Full of "good fruits" means that when you follow the wisdom from God, you are doing things that honor God and help others. When we read and study God's Word, we learn about Him and the things He wants us to know. In today's Bible verse, James describes how we can know the difference between what sounds right and what God says is right.

Wisdom that is from above or from God is pure. That means it is true and not based on someone's opinion. It is peace-loving, not always being part of an argument. It is gentle, compliant, and full of mercy.

Wisdom demonstrates thoughts and actions that treat other people with kindness and respect even when they don't deserve it. God's wisdom is unwavering, and God treats everyone equally. His truth is the same today as it has always been.

BONFIRE PRAYERS

Write a prayer to God asking Him to help you understand the wisdom from His Word.

*Thank God for the wisdom He shows
you when you study His Word.*

9

So my word that comes from my mouth will not return to me empty, but it will accomplish what I please and will prosper in what I send it to do.—Isaiah 55:11

Trevor helped his dad carry the family's suitcases into the hotel room. Trevor was so excited about all the fun things his family planned to do over the next few days. Dad suggested that Trevor put some of his things in the drawer of the bedside table. When Trevor opened the drawer, he found a Bible and showed it to his dad. "Do you think someone forgot this, or does it belong to the hotel?"

Dad hung some things in the closet and then looked to see what Trevor had. "Oh, there's a group of people who place Bibles in hotel rooms. I've heard many great stories about people who found one of those Bibles and read it. The verses they read helped them during some difficult times."

"Wow," Trevor said. "I know the Bible teaches us lots of important things, but I didn't think about how it might help someone."

"God promised that His Word would accomplish everything He wants it to, including helping people," Dad said. "God's Word helps me often!"

BEACHCOMBING FINDS

Look up the Bible verses listed on each seashell. Then on the sand pails, list one or more times that verse might help you.

Psalm
56:3

1 Timothy
4:12

Proverbs
17:17

Thank God for a verse in
His Word that helps you.

10

For the word of God is living and effective and sharper than any double-edged sword.—Hebrews 4:12

Tatum and Kayleigh were watching some music videos. They were taking turns choosing their favorites. Tatum chose a Christian music video. "The lyrics of this song have one of my favorite Bible verses," Tatum explained. "It really helps me when I feel sad."

When it was Kayleigh's turn, she chose one of her favorite groups. "I know this isn't one of your Christian songs," Kayleigh said. "But these guys are great singers. They talk about God sometimes, but they say a lot of the Bible is outdated."

Tatum thought for a moment because she wanted to be kind but tell the truth. "I understand why they might think that. But I believe the whole Bible is God's Word, and I'm learning more all the time. The Bible is called the 'living' Word of God because you can always discover something fresh to help you. I trust God to help me learn what I need to know."

"Really?" asked Kayleigh thoughtfully. "Maybe you could show me what you like to read in the Bible. I don't know where to start."

Use the flying disc code to discover today's message!

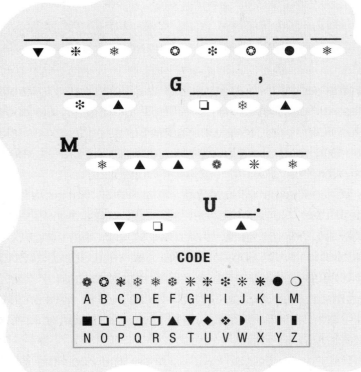

Thank God for continuing to teach you new things from His Word.

11

For whatever was written in the past was written for our instruction, so that we may have hope through endurance and through the encouragement from the Scriptures.—Romans 15:4

Some people think that parts of the Bible can be ignored. Other people think that the Bible is just a dusty old book that doesn't apply to anyone today. But if you talk to people who truly read God's Word and study the Scriptures, you'll discover most of them feel just the opposite.

God helps us understand things when He knows we need them. Sometimes we can read instructions in the Bible that help us know how to live in ways that honor God and help others. Sometimes we can read about how to have courage even when people disagree with us or when bad things happen. The Scriptures can help us have endurance (that means trusting and following God even when life is tough).

The Scriptures also give us hope. The hope the Bible gives isn't a "maybe it will happen" kind of hope, but a confidence that, if God says something, it is true. God's Word is true, it applies to all our lives, and we can trust it!

KITE WORDS

Our hope in God is a "for sure" thing, not a "maybe" thing.
Write words on the kite tail that mean "for sure."

Thank God that the Bible helps us know
about the hope we have in Him.

12

*The works of his hands are truth
and justice; all his instructions
are trustworthy.—Psalm 111:7*

Mr. Tim wrote a word in large letters on the board: TRUSTWORTHY. Turning to the group of boys he asked, "What do you think this word means?"

Lucas raised his hand and began carefully. "Well, it starts with the word 'trust,' so I'm guessing it's about trusting or believing what someone says is true."

"Great start!" Mr. Tim exclaimed. "And the 'worthy' part means someone is worthy or deserving of something. In this case, trust."

"I get it," Lucas said. "Today's Bible verse means we can believe what God says in the Bible because He is deserving of our trust."

Mr. Tim gave Lucas a big high five and exclaimed, "Great job! You are learning to study God's Word by thinking about what the verses mean."

SCRIBBLES IN THE SAND

What are some trustworthy instructions you've learned from reading the Bible? Write some of your thoughts on this page.

Sometimes we treat the Bible as if it is not important. Ask God to help you read it carefully and remember that His Words are worthy of our trust.

13

Lord, your word is forever;
it is firmly fixed in heaven.
—Psalm 119:89

Natalie and Kathryn had been enjoying a long bike ride through the park with their Aunt Amanda. They stopped to rest beneath a tall oak tree beside a little stream. Aunt Amanda unpacked their picnic, and the three of them laughed and talked while they ate their sandwiches. After they ate, Aunt Amanda pulled a Bible from her backpack and said, "I love to read from the Psalms when I'm enjoying time outside." She read a few verses from Psalm 119 aloud to the girls.

"What is it about being outside that makes you think about your Bible?" Natalie asked.

"I know God created all this beautiful nature, and it makes me think about Him and His Word," Aunt Amanda explained. "You see this big oak tree?" Aunt Amanda pointed up and the girls nodded. "It's been here for a very long time, but God's Word has been here even longer! It's just like the psalm I read to you said. God's Word is 'firmly fixed in heaven.' That means God will make sure we always have His Word so can learn about Him and His Son, Jesus."

BONFIRE PRAYERS

Are things changing in your life, like moving to a new house or a new school? Write a prayer telling God how you feel about those changes, then thank Him that you can depend on His Word, which never changes.

Thank God that we can know His Word is firmly fixed, never changing.

14

The grass withers, the flowers fade, but the word of our God remains forever.—Isaiah 40:8

Anthony helped his dad pull the rest of the tomato plants from their garden. Summer was over, and the plants had died. It was time to get the ground ready for next year. "It feels like we just planted these tomato plants," Anthony told his dad. "I can't believe we picked all those tomatoes, and now the plants are dead!"

Dad tossed the dried-up vines into the wheelbarrow. "Son, you'll find that happens with a lot of things. They don't last forever. It wasn't that long ago you were just a baby. Now, you're helping me do all this work in the garden. This morning, I read a Bible verse about the grass and flowers fading. Just like these tomatoes, they won't last forever. But it also said that God's Word doesn't fade. It lasts forever!"

"Really?" Anthony asked. "I like seeing things grow, and it's hard to see them die. I'm glad to know God says some things will last forever, like His Word."

"God is the great Creator, and we can look at lots of things He created to better understand Him," Dad added.

BEACHCOMBING FINDS

Plants and flowers are mentioned in many Bible verses. Look up the ones listed here, then draw a picture below of some of the images they made you think about.

Genesis
1:11

Mark
4:26–29

1 Peter
1:24–25

Thank God for the promise that
His Word will last forever.

15

"Heaven and earth will pass away, but my words will never pass away."—Matthew 24:35

Jesus is God the Son, and He knows the Bible is the truth for all times. Some of the Bible had been written before Jesus came to live on earth. Jesus often quoted from the Old Testament when He answered questions.

Jesus read and taught from the Scriptures to the people at the synagogue. He explained to His disciples how the Scriptures described the things that would happen to Him.

Jesus knew the things He said and did would be written down and would also become part of Scripture. Today, we have both the Old Testament and the New Testament.

When we study God's Word, we learn how sin came into our world and separated us from God. But most importantly, we learn how Jesus came to be our Savior and provide a way to save us from sin.

SEASIDE FUN

Solve the clues to discover words from today's Bible verse (Matthew 24:35).

ACROSS

2: Another word for world
3: to go by
5: Jesus returned to _____

DOWN

1: Letters spell out _____
4: To leave means to go _____
6: Opposite of always

Word Bank: HEAVEN NEVER WORDS PASS EARTH AWAY

God helps us understand the truth in His Word a little at a time. Pray that God will help you understand what He wants you to know today.

[Jesus said], "For truly I tell you, until heaven and earth pass away, not the smallest letter or one stroke of a letter will pass away from the law until all things are accomplished."—Matthew 5:18

Sara asked her mom a question while they were unloading the dishwasher. "Some of my friends and I were talking about things the Bible says will happen. They weren't sure it was true. Will the things the Bible tells about really happen?"

"Yes! In fact, many things the prophets told about in the Old Testament have already happened," Mom explained. "Jesus fulfilled lots of those prophecies. And you can be sure that the things the Bible says will happen in the future will happen. Jesus said that everything would be fulfilled, right down to the 'smallest letter.' That means the prophecy that seemed like it didn't even matter. If God says something is going to happen, it's going to happen—both the things that seem impossible and the things that seem insignificant. You see, much of the Old Testament was written in Hebrew. The smallest letter is called a *yod*. Jesus said all of God's plans will happen, even to the tiniest *yod*."

Sara thought about what her mom said, then replied, "That's what I thought. It makes me want to read my Bible even more to know about the promises God has made."

KITE WORDS

When God makes promises, He keeps them! When you think about God's promises, what words come to your mind? Write them on the tail of the kite.

Ask God to help you trust that
He keeps His promises.

17

[Paul] speaks about these things in all his letters. There are some things hard to understand in them. The untaught and unstable will twist them to their own destruction, as they also do with the rest of the Scriptures.—2 Peter 3:16

Kenan finished reading a chapter in his Bible. He was trying to read one chapter a day. Today, however, the chapter had been hard to understand. He blew out a long breath as he closed his Bible and flopped back in his chair.

"What's all that about?" his sister Anya asked.

"I read the Bible because I want to read it. But sometimes I just don't get it!" Kenan exclaimed.

"Would you believe Peter felt the same way about Paul's letters?" Anya laughed. "I just read that part this morning. When Peter was writing the book 2 Peter, he said that some of the things Paul wrote are hard to understand. And Paul wrote lots of books of the Bible!"

Kenan laughed. "Good to know. I guess if even Peter thought it was hard, I'll just keep hanging in there and ask God to help me understand."

SCRIBBLES IN THE SAND

Do you have questions when you read the Bible? Write some of the questions you've had recently in the sand below.

It's okay to tell God when you don't understand something you read in the Bible. Talk to God about it. God will keep teaching you about the Bible for the rest of your life!

18

If anyone takes away from the words of the book of this prophecy, God will take away his share of the tree of life and the holy city, which are written about in this book.—Revelation 22:19

Revelation is the last book in the Bible. It was written by the apostle John while he was in exile on the island of Patmos. Exile means that he was forced to move away from his home and live somewhere else.

Many people read Revelation to learn about things that will happen in the future. However, John also wrote to remind believers that Jesus is our Lord and Savior and that eventually, evil will be destroyed, and God will reign in His kingdom forever.

John was in exile because he was a follower of Jesus. At that time the government of Rome was persecuting Christians. That means believers were harassed or even punished for claiming to be Christians. John wrote to warn and encourage believers not to give up.

One of the last verses in Revelation (22:19) warns us not to change anything in the Bible. We can't take away the parts we don't like or change things to make us feel better or fit in with the culture more. God's Word is truth. It will last forever.

BONFIRE PRAYERS

If you are a Christian, write a prayer asking God to help you have the courage to let people know you have trusted in Jesus as your Savior. If you aren't a Christian yet, ask God to help you understand more about what becoming a Christian means.

Thank God for the truth you can learn in His Word.

19

Do you not know? Have you not heard? The Lord is the everlasting God, the Creator of the whole earth. He never becomes faint or weary; there is no limit to his understanding.—Isaiah 40:28

Koda's mom picked him up from his friend's house after school. When Koda got in the car, his mom could tell he had something on his mind. "What's wrong, Koda?" she asked.

"Some of the guys were talking about different people worshiping different gods," Koda explained. "I said there is only one true God, and they laughed and said I didn't know everything."

Mom nodded and said, "The Bible said that believers would experience just what you did. You will meet people who believe differently. But never let that cause you to give up what you know is true. We know that God is the one true God. He has always been and will always be God. He is the Creator of all we know. Be kind to your friends, but don't stop sharing what you know is true. Let's pray for your friends."

BEACHCOMBING FINDS

Many of the psalms celebrate God for who He is. Locate Psalm 145 in your Bible. On each beach rock, write something that each verse tells you about who God is.

Psalm 145:1

Psalm 145:3

Psalm 145:9

Psalm 145:18

Psalm 145:13

Ask God to help you have the faith to know that He is the one true God.

20

This is what the Lord, the King of Israel and its Redeemer, the Lord of Armies, says: I am the first and I am the last. There is no God but me.—Isaiah 44:6

Carly turned to a new page in her journal. Her Bible study teacher had challenged the class to make a list of words and names that describe God. Her teacher explained that the names used to describe God in the Bible could help them understand more about who God is.

Carly found several names and descriptive words in her verse for the day, Isaiah 44:6. After reading and thinking about the verse, she wrote at the top of the page, "The one and only God."

Carly understood some of the words like "King" and "Lord." She wrote those in her journal and added notes about what she thought those words meant. She didn't understand some of the words like "Redeemer" and "Lord of Armies."

She was excited to take her list to next week's Bible study and ask her teacher about them.

SEASIDE FUN

As you read words in the Bible that describe God, you will learn more about Him. Can you find these words in the word search below?

Word Bank: REDEEMER LORD KING ETERNAL PROTECTOR
CREATOR FAITHFUL GOOD KIND LOVE

G	R	K	D	M	C	L	T	E	Z
F	P	E	T	E	R	N	A	L	D
R	A	R	M	K	P	K	O	D	C
Q	E	I	O	W	Q	I	E	E	R
J	K	D	T	T	U	N	Q	L	E
S	I	F	E	H	E	G	J	O	A
G	N	Q	M	E	F	C	Y	R	T
O	D	T	E	V	M	U	T	D	O
O	T	F	O	F	I	E	L	O	R
D	B	V	L	O	V	E	R	W	R

*We can praise God when we pray. Praise
Him that He is the one and only God.*

21

Now to the King eternal, immortal, invisible, the only God, be honor and glory forever and ever. Amen.—1 Timothy 1:17

Today's Bible verse helps us understand more about who God is. God is the King of all creation, both in heaven and on earth. Even more than that, He is the *eternal* King. That means God has always existed and will always continue to exist. Eternal means having no end. That's hard for us to understand because most things we know have a begin-ning and an end. But God, who created us, has always existed.

Immortal is another word that means never-ending. *Invisible* sounds mysterious. It means that we can't see God. But we can look at the things He has done, talk to people who are Christians, and read His Word (the Bible) to learn about Him.

This verse also tells us how we should respect God. We give God honor and glory forever and ever. When we trust in Jesus as our Savior, we have the promise that we will live with Him forever. That means we can truly give honor and glory to God forever!

KITE WORDS

What are some ways you can honor God? Write some of your ideas on the tail of the kite.

Talk to God about how amazing He is.
Thank Him that He is the eternal God.

22

The LORD—the LORD is a compassionate and gracious God, slow to anger and abounding in faithful love and truth.—Exodus 34:6

Jayden dropped his backpack on the kitchen table and grabbed a drink from the refrigerator. His older sister was making a sandwich. "What's wrong?" she asked. "You seem out of sorts."

Jayden sat down at the table and put his head in his hands. "Did you ever have one of those days when it felt like you messed up everything?" His sister nodded and sat down with him. Jayden explained, "I forgot about a paper that was due today. That made me mad, and I took it out on my best friend. Then I dropped my phone on the way home and cracked the screen. I keep thinking I've done something to make God really mad at me."

"Jayden," his sister said. "God is not like that. You've had a bad day, but the Bible says God is slow to anger and filled with love for us. Sometimes our emotions get out of control, but God never does. He loves us even when we feel unlovable."

SCRIBBLES IN THE SAND

Write about some times when you feel like God might be upset with you then thank Him for the way He loves you anyway.

You can tell God how you're feeling, even when you're angry. He knows anyway.

23

Every good and perfect gift is from above, coming down from the Father of lights, who does not change like shifting shadows.—James 1:17

Sophia's family gathered to pray before bedtime. Sophia always enjoyed this special time with her family. The TV and all electronics were turned off, and it felt so peaceful. Sometimes her parents or sisters would ask for prayer for a friend or a test at school. Then, each night a different family member would pray. Tonight was Mom's turn.

Before Mom prayed, she placed a large blue glass bowl on the table. "This will be our thankful bowl," Mom explained. "For the next month, I want us to really pay attention to all the things we can be thankful to God for. Here's a stack of paper strips and a couple of pencils. Write what you are thankful for on the paper and leave it in the bowl. In a month, we'll have a prayer night when we are simply thankful to God. We'll read all the papers and then thank God together."

Sophia knew the first thing she would write on one of the paper strips. She was thankful to God for her family.

BONFIRE PRAYERS

You can write your own "Thankful List." Start your list today and add to it as many times as you like.

God,
I am thankful
to You for . . .

Think back over the last day.
Thank God for at least three things.

24

*God is not a man, that he might lie, or a
son of man, that he might change his mind.
Does he speak and not act, or promise
and not fulfill?—Numbers 23:19*

Henry and Grandpa sat down under a tree to rest after they finished mowing the yard. Henry surprised Grandpa with a question. "Has God ever let you down?"

Grandpa looked at Henry and replied, "Sometimes God hasn't answered the way I wanted Him to, but He has never let me down. Why do you ask? I'm guessing there is a reason."

"Well, sometimes people break promises or say they'll do one thing but then do another," Henry explained. "And last week, my best friend lied to me. Does God ever lie?"

Grandpa replied, "God is not like your friend, Henry. He isn't like you or me either! Because of sin, we don't always do things the way we should. But God does not sin as humans do, He never lies, and He never changes His mind. He is God! You can believe that when God promises something He will keep it. When He says something, He is telling the truth. He will do what He says He will do."

BEACHCOMBING FINDS

Some people use metal detectors to find things on the beach. Locate five coins partially hidden in the sand. Look up the verse referenced on each coin and write beside the coin the promise from God that you discover.

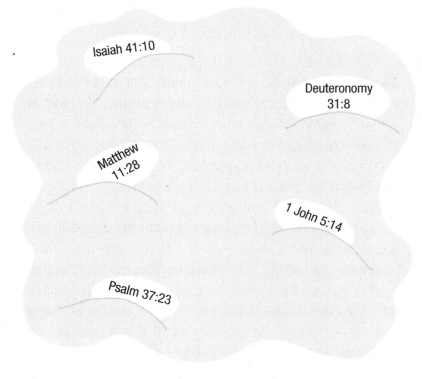

Isaiah 41:10

Deuteronomy 31:8

Matthew 11:28

1 John 5:14

Psalm 37:23

Ask God to help you trust Him even when you're not sure what He is doing.

25

Indeed, the Protector of Israel does not slumber or sleep.—Psalm 121:4

Abigail and Amelia shared a room. They often read for a while before turning out the light at night. "I'm sort of scared sometimes right after we turn out the light. It gets so dark," Abigail said softly.

"You know, you can pray to God about it," Amelia said as she fluffed her pillow.

"But God has so many more important things to take care of than a girl who's a little scared of the dark," Abigail answered in a small voice.

Amelia smiled as she pulled up the covers. "I read Psalm 121 every night before I turn out the light. It reminds me that God never sleeps. He doesn't need sleep! And because He is God, He knows everything that's happening all the time. Even when one of those things is a girl who's a little scared," Amelia replied with a wink.

SEASIDE FUN

Solve the code below to find another great truth from Psalm 121. After you solve the code, locate Psalm 121 in your Bible and read the whole chapter. It's only eight verses!

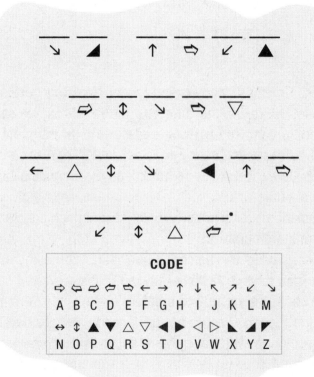

MY HELP COMES FROM THE LORD.

Thank God that He is always awake and aware of you. Even if you wake up in the middle of the night, you can talk to God.

26

In the beginning God created the heavens and the earth.—Genesis 1:1

Noah Timothy!" Mom called loudly from the back door. It was time for dinner, and she didn't see Noah as she glanced around the yard. She stepped onto the patio and saw Noah kneeling near her flower bed. "What is so interesting there, Noah? You're hardly moving a muscle."

"It's a caterpillar," Noah whispered back excitedly, without looking up. "It's making a chrysalis. I think it's going to be a monarch butterfly."

Mom smiled as she shook her head. "You enjoy nature more than anyone I've ever known. I love how you like to learn about the world God created."

"God's world is so amazing!" Noah exclaimed. "Will you take a picture with your phone so I can keep track of its progress? I'm going to look it up online and see what else I can learn about butterflies!"

KITE WORDS

Today's Kite Word is CREATION. List some of your favorite parts of creation on the kite tail.

Thank God for some of your favorite things in creation.

27

God blessed them: "Be fruitful, multiply, and fill the waters of the seas, and let the birds multiply on the earth."—Genesis 1:22

Are you surprised when you see the moon and stars at night? Are you shocked when a wave rolls onto the shore? What about when it rains on a spring day? These things probably don't surprise you because they are normal parts of creation. You probably know what to expect during wintertime or summertime where you live. In school, you may have studied about the life cycles of certain plants or animals. It can be very fascinating!

When God created the world and everything in it, He didn't stop there. God's command to "be fruitful and multiply" was part of His process of creation. He made all living things to produce more living things just like them. Because of sin, our world is not the perfect place it was when God created it. Things die or get diseases or harm each other. But God is in control. We still have daytime and nighttime. We have seasons, sunshine, and rain. Our world keeps spinning around the sun. We know when each full moon will happen, and we know which days will have more or less sunlight. God shows His faithfulness through creation.

SCRIBBLES IN THE SAND

List one of God's creatures (like a sea turtle, seal, or gull) and then list some of the ways God provides for that creature. Think about how God provides similar things for you.

Talk to God about something in creation that makes you think of Him.

28

Acknowledge that the L<small>ORD</small> is God. He made us, and we are his—his people, the sheep of his pasture.—Psalm 100:3

Lily skipped out the back door toward the barn. She was spending a week with her aunt and uncle on their sheep farm. She was so excited. Uncle Richard said that a new lamb had been born that morning, and she could come see it after lunch. Lily cautiously peered into the barn and saw her uncle in one of the stalls.

"Come in and have a look," Uncle Richard said. "She's a cutie."

"Aww, look, how sweet!" Lily exclaimed. She looked around at all the things hanging on the walls and organized around the barn. "Do you need all of this to take care of sheep?" she asked.

Uncle Richard laughed. "We sure do. Taking care of sheep is a lot of work. I guess that's why my favorite parts to read in the Bible are about sheep. Those verses remind me that we are the sheep of God's pasture. He takes care of us like we take care of these sheep."

BONFIRE PRAYERS

Psalm 23 is sometimes called "The Shepherd's Psalm." Did you know you can use Scripture as prayer? Locate Psalm 23 in your Bible. Copy your favorite part here as a prayer to God.

Thank God for the many ways
He cares for you.

29

The pottery class was about to start. Charlie was so excited. He had often visited Mrs. Tracy's shop. He loved the beautiful things she made. When Mrs. Tracy said she was offering a class, Charlie begged his mom to let him sign up.

As time went on, Charlie was surprised to realize how hard it was and how many times they had to take the clay and start over. "How long did it take you to get so good?" Charlie asked Mrs. Tracy.

She laughed and took two small bowls from the shelf. One was lopsided and a bit funny looking. The other was one of the prettiest bowls Charlie had seen. "I keep these to remind myself how far I've come with years of practice and patience," Mrs. Tracy explained. "They also remind me that God is my potter. He made me, and He knew what He was doing from the beginning. God sees me as His masterpiece. He sees you the same way, Charlie."

BEACHCOMBING FINDS

Locate Ephesians 2:10 in your Bible. This verse also talks about how we are the works of God's hands. Finish each phrase in the sand dollars based on what you read in Ephesians 2:10.

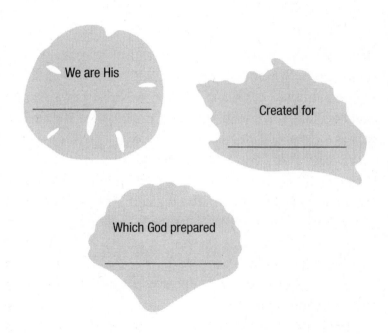

We are His

_____

Created for

_____

Which God prepared

_____

Ask God to help you realize that
you are His masterpiece.

30

Give thanks to the L<small>ORD</small>, for he is good; his faithful love endures forever.—Psalm 107:1

Victoria," Mom said, "take this bag of cookies over to Mrs. Martin. She's been very sick, but I can see her sitting in the sun in her backyard. Tell her we've been praying for her. And here's a cookie for you to eat on the way," Mom added as she winked.

Victoria loved the smell of fresh-baked cookies. She was still nibbling on the cookie when she walked over to Mrs. Martin. "Mom just made cookies. She said to bring you some and tell you we've been praying for you," Victoria said, smiling.

"Oh, how sweet!" Mrs. Martin exclaimed. "God is so good! I was just sitting here thinking about how good some fresh-baked cookies would taste."

"Really?" Victoria asked, surprised.

"Oh, yes," Mrs. Martin assured her. "God is always good. Even though I've been sick, I know He is caring for me. Thank you so much for praying for me!"

SEASIDE FUN

Use today's Bible verse (Psalm 107:1) to solve the crossword clues.

DOWN

1: Today's Bible verse is found in _____ 107:1.
3: God's love endures _____.
4: God is _____.

ACROSS

2: God's love is _____.
4: _____ thanks to the Lord.

Word Bank: FOREVER GOOD PSALM GIVE FAITHFUL

Thank God for the many ways He shows His goodness to you.

31

Then Job replied to the Lord: I know that you can do anything and no plan of yours can be thwarted.—Job 42:1–2

Some people think that following God means everything should be great and nothing bad will happen. The truth is that everyone experiences good times *and* bad times. When you are a Christian, you have a relationship with Jesus. You know God will be with you to rejoice with you in good times and help you in bad times.

There's a book in the Old Testament about a man named Job. He loved and followed God, but he still experienced terrible things. Some of his friends tried to talk with him. It was nice that they came, but they began to share their own wisdom with Job, and they were wrong. Job wondered why God would allow him to go through such a bad time, and he called out to God in despair.

God helped Job realize that only God is God. God knows things we don't. Even when we don't understand why something bad is happening to us, we can trust that God has a plan and that His plan will succeed.

KITE WORDS

Trust means to be assured of someone or something. Trust in God means putting our confidence in Him. Think about today's Kite Word, TRUST. Then list times when it is hard to trust on the kite trail.

Ask God to help you trust Him even when you don't understand why things happen.

32

"The Lord your God is among you, a warrior who saves. He will rejoice over you with gladness. He will be quiet in his love. He will delight in you with singing."—Zephaniah 3:17

The porch swing squeaked softly as Lainey and Mimi rocked back and forth. Lainey closed her eyes and listened to Mimi sing the songs she often sang when it was time to be quiet for a bit. "Mimi," Lainey said sleepily, "I feel so safe when I'm near you and listening to your voice."

Mimi gave her a little hug and said, "That makes my heart happy. Do you know what? I love you so much that my heart feels happy. Did you know the Bible tells us that God delights in us and sings about us? God doesn't need us to make Him happy, but He loves us so much that it brings Him joy."

"Really?" Lainey asked. "I know God makes me happy, but I didn't know God loves me so much that it makes Him happy too."

SCRIBBLES IN THE SAND

God made you, and that's one reason why you make Him happy. In the scribble space below, write why God makes you happy.

Ask God to help you understand the many ways you make Him happy.

33

For you, Lord, are kind and ready to forgive, abounding in faithful love to all who call on you.—Psalm 86:5

Aunt Cindy and Mom were looking through a calendar, trying to pick a week for their combined family vacation to the beach. "I can't do that week," Aunt Cindy said. "I'm on call that week, but I could do the next week."

"What does 'on call' mean?" Jackson asked his aunt.

"Well, Jackson, since I am a nurse, it means for that week I have to be available all the time if a patient has an emergency and needs me," Aunt Cindy explained.

"That sounds overwhelming!" Jackson exclaimed. "Don't you get tired?"

"It can be overwhelming," Aunt Cindy agreed. "That's why our nursing group takes turns. We have to have a break. God is the only one who can always be 'on call.' I am so thankful He is always available because I call on Him often, especially to help me help others."

BONFIRE PRAYERS

Today's Bible verse gives us some ideas about things we can pray. Add a sentence after each of the prayer starters below.

Lord, You are kind . . .

_____

You are always ready to forgive . . .

_____

You abound in faithful love . . .

_____

Thank You that I can call on You to . . .

_____

Thank God that He is always available to us, even when it is not an emergency.

34

In the beginning was the Word, and the Word was with God, and the Word was God.—John 1:1

Christmas is when we remember the birth of Jesus. But did you know that Jesus is God the Son, and God the Son existed long before He came to earth as a human baby? He is eternal. That means God the Son has always existed and will exist forever. In one of his books of the Bible, Jesus's friend John describes Jesus as "the Word"?

Even though Jesus is God, He came to earth to live with us and experience things the way we do. Jesus did this because of His great love for us.

When we pray to Jesus, He knows how we feel because He experienced those kinds of things too. Jesus is with us not only in our present time, but He also will be with us forever because He is God. He has always existed, and He always will exist. We can count on Him forever!

BEACHCOMBING FINDS

Look up each of these Bible verses. What clues do you find that remind you that God the Father, Son, and Holy Spirit were all there during creation?

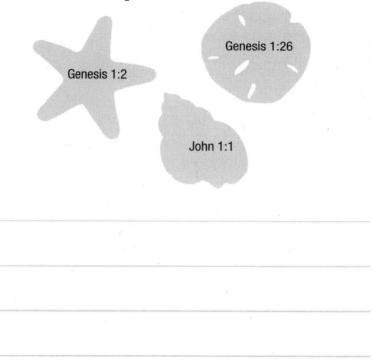

Genesis 1:26

Genesis 1:2

John 1:1

_____

_____

_____

_____

Thank Jesus that He knows exactly what you are thinking and feeling and loves you no matter what.

35

*"For God loved the world in this way:
He gave his one and only Son, so that
everyone who believes in him will not perish
but have eternal life."—John 3:16*

Harper and Aria were practicing their memory verse for Bible club. "This is an easy one," Harper said happily. "I think it's the first Bible verse I ever memorized." Harper quickly rattled off the words of John 3:16, then bowed with a flourish.

Aria seemed a little embarrassed and said, "I'm new to church and so is my mom. I'm just beginning to learn how to memorize Bible verses. Can you help me understand what this verse means? Maybe that will help me memorize the words."

Surprised, Harper thought. Then she said, "I got so busy memorizing the words, I didn't even think about what it means. Let's look at each part of the verse and talk about it."

Together the girls talked about why God sent His Son, Jesus, to earth to take the punishment for their sins. They talked about how trusting in Jesus gives the promise of eternal life.

SEASIDE FUN

Find words from the word bank in today's word search. Try to say today's Bible verse, John 3:16, using only these words as a prompt.

Word Bank: GOD LOVED WORLD GAVE ONLY SON EVERYONE BELIEVES ETERNAL LIFE

```
E W U V X M Q A E F
V O G W J S C L H G
E R B E L I E V E S
R L S E B U P E L U
Y D O T C N Q I I L
O L N E A Y G C F O
N P G R R E A Y E V
E O G N F M V N Y E
G Z O A X M E H L D
J Y D L F H O N L Y
```

Ask God to help you understand the amazing message of love found in John 3:16.

36

"This is eternal life: that they may know you, the only true God, and the one you have sent—Jesus Christ."—John 17:3

Let's begin today's Bible study with a little review," Mr. Vincent began. "We know that God is the Creator, and the world He created was good. Then what happened?"

"People sinned," Logan answered. "And sin broke the relationship between people and God."

"Very good," Mr. Vincent said, nodding encouragingly. "But even as early as Genesis, chapter 3, what did God promise to do about this broken relationship?"

"Oh, I know that one!" Eric responded. "God promised to send someone who would defeat Satan. That someone is Jesus."

"Great job, boys!" Mr. Vincent encouraged. "And why did God fulfill that promise?"

Nathan quickly replied, "Because God wants people to have a right relationship with Him. He wants us to be able to live eternally with Him."

KITE WORDS

You are beginning to learn more and more about Jesus. Write on the kite tail some of the things you know about Jesus.

***Thank God for sending His Son, Jesus,
so we can have eternal life.***

37

Jesus came near and said to them, "All authority has been given to me in heaven and on earth."—Matthew 28:18

"What did Jesus mean when He said all authority had been given to Him?" Kiara asked her dad.

"Do you know what authority means?" Dad asked. Kiara shook her head no, so Dad continued. "You can think of authority as power. A person in authority can influence thoughts or command behavior. A person in authority is in control."

"So, Jesus has the power to cause things to happen here on earth and in heaven," Kiara said thoughtfully. "He is God, and He can do the things God does."

"Very good," Dad said encouragingly. "And we can trust Jesus's authority because He is God, and He loves us."

Kiara thought about all that she had been reading in the book of Matthew. Jesus had said and commanded so many things. Now, she wanted to go back and read them again with Jesus's authority in mind. She was excited to learn more about what it might mean for her life that Jesus is in control.

SCRIBBLES IN THE SAND

Write down some of your thoughts as you ponder the fact that Jesus has the power of God.

Ask God to help you understand more about Jesus's authority.

38

[Jesus] answered, "It is written: Man must not live on bread alone but on every word that comes from the mouth of God."—Matthew 4:4

We learned in the last devotional that Jesus has all authority in heaven and on earth. We know Jesus is far more powerful than Satan. But did you know that Satan actually tried to tempt Jesus to do wrong? Jesus could have simply said to Satan, "Go away!" Instead, Jesus used God's Word to resist Satan. He knew the Scriptures in His heart and said them back to Satan.

One of those temptations happened after Jesus had been fasting for forty days. Fasting means not eating because the person is focusing on praying. Jesus was hungry, so Satan tried to tempt Jesus to turn rocks into bread. You can read Jesus's response in today's Bible verse.

The part of the Bible we know as the Old Testament was around during Jesus's lifetime. Jesus said all Scripture is the Word of God. Jesus used Scripture to resist temptation. Jesus set the example for us. We can remember Scripture when we are tempted to do wrong or even when we're not sure what to do.

BONFIRE PRAYERS

Many Bible verses can be used as prayers. Look up the following verses and read it as a prayer to God. Write your prayer in the space below the verse reference.

Isaiah 25:1

Psalm 103:1–5

2 Chronicles 7:14

Ask God to help you remember verses from Scripture whenever you are tempted.

39

Then beginning with Moses and all the Prophets, he [Jesus] interpreted for them the things concerning himself in all the Scriptures.—Luke 24:27

Liam had just started going to church with his friend, Wyatt. One Sunday, Liam asked, "Did Jesus have a Bible?"

Wyatt knew his friend was just beginning to learn about Jesus. He wanted to encourage Liam, so he tried to answer with kindness and encouragement. "They didn't have Bibles like we have now. The Scriptures were written on scrolls or rolled-up parchment. The New Testament had not been written yet because they were living it! But they had the Old Testament. They called those Scriptures the Law, the Psalms, and the Prophets."

"So Jesus knew about all of that Scripture?" Liam asked.

Wyatt smiled and replied, "Jesus knew it and often read from it or quoted from it. The day Jesus rose from the dead, He even had a long conversation with a couple of guys, and He explained how all the Law and the Prophets had been about His coming and the things that happened. I'll show you where that story is after church. It's one of my favorites!"

BEACHCOMBING FINDS

The story of "The Emmaus Disciples" is very interesting. Locate Luke 24:13–35 and read the story. Can you answer each of the questions on the beach after combing through this story?

How many disciples were traveling to Emmaus?

_____

Who began to walk with them that they didn't recognize?

_____

What is one thing the disciples told Jesus when they thought He was just another traveler?

_____

_____

When did the disciples recognize that the man was Jesus?

_____

_____

What kinds of things did Jesus tell them about?

_____

_____

Everyone begins learning about the Bible at different times. Ask God to help you be patient with people who are just discovering His Word.

40

"For God did not send his Son into the world to condemn the world, but to save the world through him."—John 3:17

Mom," Charlotte began while helping her mother with dinner, "some of the girls were talking at lunch, and one of them said that God is just waiting for us to mess up so He can zap us."

Mom kept peeling potatoes and asked, "Is that what you think?"

"Not really," Charlotte replied. "I know God doesn't like it when we sin, but I remember a Bible verse that says He is gracious and ready to forgive our sins. That doesn't sound like He's out to get us."

"Good answer!" Mom said with a big smile. "This is why it is so important to know God's Word—so that you know the truth. You are going to hear people you know say a lot of things that sound true but aren't. The only way you'll know the truth is by knowing what God said in the Bible. That's what you just did, and I'm very proud of you."

SEASIDE FUN

John 3:17 tells us important information. It tells us one thing Jesus did not come to do and one thing Jesus came to do. Use the code to discover these two answers.

JESUS DID NOT COME TO

___ ___ ___ ___ ___ ___ ___

THE WORLD; JESUS CAME TO

___ ___ ___ ___ THE WORLD.

CODE

✔	🚲	☐	🛡	🎁	🚌	⬛	🛗	ⓘ	➤	✸	✈	❗
A	B	C	D	E	F	G	H	I	J	K	L	M

👁	👂	🚄	()	✗	?	🛶	🏠	🚆	⌇	⊘	⊖	⊗
N	O	P	Q	R	S	T	U	V	W	X	Y	Z

Thank God for the truth that Jesus came to be the Savior of the world.

41

*For Christ also suffered for sins once for all,
the righteous for the unrighteous, that he might
bring you to God. He was put to death in the flesh
but made alive by the Spirit.—1 Peter 3:18*

Mateo was trying to understand what it meant that Jesus died for our sins. He knew his papa could explain it. "Papa, I know the facts about how Jesus died for our sins and rose again. But I still don't understand why. Why did Jesus have to die? How did that fix anything?"

Mateo's papa sat down beside him and put his arm around him. "I'm glad you want to understand, Mateo. That is a good thing. You see, everyone who has ever lived, except Jesus, has sinned. Jesus came to earth to take our punishment, and He could only do that by living a sinless life. Which He did!

"Because of sin, we all deserve the wrath of God. But Jesus took our punishment once and for all! Accepting this free gift of love and forgiveness from Jesus restores our relationship with our God. And Jesus's resurrection proved His power over sin and death! He lives so we, too, can live with Him forever."

KITE WORDS

First Peter 3:18 says Jesus Christ is "the righteous for the unrighteous." Righteous means doing right or someone who does the right things. All the things Jesus did were righteous, because He obeyed God the Father. On the kite tail, list some of the things Jesus did.

RIGHTEOUS

Thank Jesus for taking our punishment so we can be made right with God.

42

For the wages of sin is death, but the gift of God is eternal life in Christ Jesus our Lord.—Romans 6:23

You've read about how God created a good world. Then, Adam and Eve gave in to temptation and disobeyed God. This is called *sin*, and since then, all people have sinned. God provided the solution He promised. He sent His one and only Son to live a human life, but never sin. Jesus resisted all temptations and willingly gave His life to take on the punishment we deserve.

We all deserve eternal punishment, but because of Jesus's sacrifice, we are offered the free gift of forgiveness and the promise of eternal life. Because it is a gift, we can't earn it. When you are given a gift, all you must do is receive it. When you realize that you are a sinner and you need the forgiveness Jesus offers, admit to God that you're a sinner and that you believe in His Son, Jesus. Tell God and others that you trust in Jesus as your Savior.

SCRIBBLES IN THE SAND

When you know you are ready to trust Jesus and become a Christian, or when you want to explain it to someone else, use the information scribbled in the sand to help you know what to do or say. Locate the verses in your Bible and put a check mark beside each verse after you read it.

Admit – Admit to God that you are a sinner. Repent, turning away from your sin. (Romans 3:23)

Believe – Believe that Jesus is God's Son and receive God's gift of forgiveness from sin. (Ephesians 2:8-9)

Confess – Confess your faith in Jesus Christ as Savior and Lord. (Romans 10:9-10, 13)

If you have already trusted in Jesus as Savior, thank Him for saving you. If you haven't, ask God to help you understand what trusting in Jesus means.

43

If we confess our sins, he [God] is faithful and righteous to forgive us our sins and to cleanse us from all unrighteousness.—1 John 1:9

Maria was nervous about talking to her cousin, Ava, about becoming a Christian. Maria had prayed for Ava for a long time. One day, Ava started the conversation. She noticed Maria reading her Bible and asked her why she wanted to read such an old book. Maria began to explain what she had learned about Jesus and that His love was as real today as it was back in Bible times. Maria explained how sin had messed up our relationship with God, but how God had sent Jesus to be our Savior.

Ava sadly shook her head and said, "I'm afraid God wouldn't forgive me. I've done some bad things that I'm too embarrassed to talk about."

Maria smiled as she replied, "But that's the wonderful thing. God knows everything, so He's never surprised. First John 1:9 says God is faithful. He will forgive our sins and make us righteous. That means we can be right with God again!"

BONFIRE PRAYERS

Write down some things you need God to forgive you for. It might be cheating on a test, being a bully toward someone, or having a wrong attitude. As you pray and ask God to forgive you, draw a big X through the words. Thank God for His forgiveness.

God can forgive anything you have done.
You can talk to Him about anything.

44

*If you confess with your mouth, "Jesus is Lord,"
and believe in your heart that God raised him
from the dead, you will be saved.—Romans 10:9*

Nolan was walking home from baseball practice with his older brother, Kameron. "Hey, Kam," Nolan asked, "You got saved last year, right?"

"I did," Kam replied. "Why? What's up?"

"I've been thinking about the word *saved*," Nolan explained. "I know when we were hiking and I almost fell off that cliff, you grabbed my shirt and saved me from falling. But what does becoming a Christian have to do with being saved? Does it mean you'll never get hurt?"

"Oh, I get what you're asking," Kam answered. "Trusting in Jesus as Savior is what we call becoming a Christian. It is also called being saved because we are saved, or rescued, from spending an eternity separated from God."

"Hmm," Nolan said thoughtfully. "That makes sense. I may have more questions later."

Kam laughed and ruffled his little brother's hair. "Ask anytime. I'm glad you're asking questions."

BEACHCOMBING FINDS

Becoming a Christian means you are saved or rescued from separation from God for eternity. It also means that God the Holy Spirit is with you to help you each day of your life. Now that you know what *saved* means, look up the Bible verses listed on the shells. Put a check mark beside each Bible verse reference after you find and read the verse.

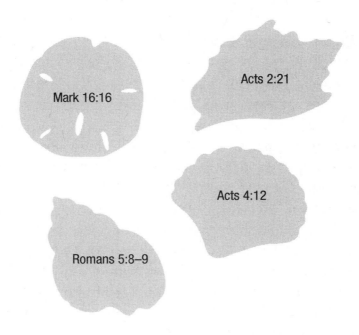

Mark 16:16

Acts 2:21

Acts 4:12

Romans 5:8–9

Thank God for Jesus, who came
to be our Savior and Lord.

45

For everyone who calls on the name of the Lord will be saved.—Romans 10:13

Chloe had been thinking about something she heard at church. The pastor talked about how anyone could become a Christian, but not everyone is a Christian. Finally, she decided to ask her mom. "Mom, if everyone is invited to be saved, why isn't everyone a Christian?"

"Jesus did come to be the Savior of the world," Mom explained, "but the Bible also helps us know that salvation is a gift we must accept. Sadly, it's a choice not everyone makes. Some people don't think they need salvation. And others think they can be saved by someone other than Jesus. We can't make anyone believe, but it's our responsibility to share the good news with everybody."

Chloe slowly nodded her head. "I get it. God doesn't turn anyone away who chooses to receive His gift of forgiveness. I think I understand better now."

SEASIDE FUN

Jesus came to be the Savior of all those who trust in Him.
Solve the crossword to discover some of those "everyone"
groups of people.

Word Bank: KIDS
NEIGHBORS ADULTS
EVERYONE FRIENDS
FAMILY

DOWN

1: Salvation is for _____ who believes.
2: _____ are people you know and like to spend time with.
5: Another word for grown-ups is _____.

ACROSS

3: People who live near you are your _____.
4: People who are related to you
6: People who are younger than adults are _____.

**Thank God that He is ready and willing to
welcome all who call on His name.**

46

Jesus told him, "I am the way, the truth, and the life. No one comes to the Father except through me."—John 14:6

Sometimes people get confused about what is the truth. It's easy to say things because they sound right or because someone else said it. It is important to know what the Bible says. God's Word is the truth. For example, you might hear someone say that there are many ways to get to heaven. Some people may say you have to be good enough to earn your way to God.

Their reasons may seem believable, but the Bible says we can go to heaven only by trusting in Jesus as Savior and Lord. Jesus told His disciples, "I am the way, the truth, and the life. No one comes to the Father except through me."

Jesus came to earth to live as a human, suffer for our sins, die, and be resurrected from the dead. He is the only way for us to have eternal life.

KITE WORDS

What are some things you have heard people say about how to get to heaven? The kite has the words "One Way." Jesus is the only way. On the tail, write other ways people think you can get to heaven, and then draw an X through each of those ways.

Ask God to help you recognize whether what someone says is the truth or not.

47

Do not misuse the name of the LORD your God, because the LORD will not leave anyone unpunished who misuses his name.—Exodus 20:7

Colton," Aunt Melissa said while they were putting away the gardening tools. "I appreciate your helping me get my flowers planted, but I need to talk to you about something."

"Sure, what do you need?" Colton asked.

"Well," Aunt Melissa began carefully. "When you spilled the bag of potting soil, you said Jesus's name out of frustration. Jesus is my Savior, and I want to be sure His name is respected. The Bible says Jesus's name is the only name under heaven given to people so they can be saved. I know you didn't think you were disrespecting Jesus, but it was disrespectful to Jesus, and I love you enough to tell you."

Colton thought for a bit then said, "Sorry, Aunt Melissa. The guys say it all the time, and I never thought about it. Thanks for helping me understand," he grinned, "instead of yelling at me for it."

SCRIBBLES IN THE SAND

Think about the name *Jesus*. On the sand, list reasons why Jesus's name should be treated with honor.

JESUS

Thank God that Jesus is the only one who can save you. Ask Him to help you honor Jesus's name.

48

For all have sinned and fall short of the glory of God; they are justified freely by his grace through the redemption that is in Christ Jesus.—Romans 3:23–24

Mia and Emily carried their art supplies to the table. Grandma Ruby had just gone to live at a nursing home. The girls' mom suggested they print some of Grandma Ruby's favorite Bible verses on small posters and decorate them. She explained that it would make Grandma happy to see those verses decorating the walls of her room.

Mia opened her Bible to the first Bible verses on the list, Romans 3:23–24. "I know the first part of this verse," Mia said, "but the second part is new to me. What does *justified* mean?"

"My teacher always says *justified* means 'just as if I had never sinned.' The verse means that God's mercy takes away the punishment for all of our sins. The rest of the verse means that Jesus redeemed us. That means He restored our relationship with God, which sin messed up."

"Oh, wow," Mia exclaimed. "Now I know why that's one of Grandma's favorites. I think I'll write down that one."

BONFIRE PRAYERS

Justified and *redemption* are big words. They describe how God's free gift of grace takes away the sins that separate us from Him. Write a prayer to God thanking Him that being justified means God sees you "just as if you had never sinned."

Thank God for justifying and redeeming people who believe in Him.

49

Coasts and islands, listen to me; distant peoples, pay attention. The L<small>ORD</small> called me before I was born. He named me while I was in my mother's womb.—Isaiah 49:1

Have you seen pictures or videos of rocky coasts where waves crashed against the rocks? Or have you seen islands that seem far away, surrounded by water? Have you ever wanted to climb to a tall cliff and call out, "Hey, listen to me!"?

That sounds like what Isaiah was describing in today's Bible verse. He described some of the most majestic things he could imagine and said, "Listen! God knows me, and He knew me before I was born."

The Bible teaches us the truth about God, and it also teaches us the truth about us. Yes, about you! Before you were born, God knew your name. Isn't that amazing? You are not here by accident. God knew all about you even before He created the world. Does that make you feel important to God? You are. He knows your name! He knows you!

BEACHCOMBING FINDS

God knows our name. The Bible also tells us how we should treat God's name. Locate each verse listed in the seashells. Color in the shell after you read the verse.

Psalm 145:1–2

Exodus 20:7

Deuteronomy 5:11

Psalm 103:1

Acts 2:21

Tell God how you feel when you think about how well He knows you.

50

*Now this is what the L*ord *says—the one who created you, Jacob, and the one who formed you, Israel—"Do not fear, for I have redeemed you; I have called you by your name; you are mine."—Isaiah 43:1*

Sam was feeling sorry for himself. It was school break, and everyone he knew had gone on an exciting trip or was having fun with grandparents. Sam's mom had started a new job, and Mrs. Maxwell was at the house to keep an eye on Sam and his younger sister. "I don't think I really matter to anyone," Sam muttered under his breath.

"What did you say?" Mrs. Maxwell asked as she folded towels.

"Oh, nothing," Sam mumbled. "I'm just lonely, and I'm sure no one cares."

"I am so sorry you feel that way," Mrs. Maxwell said. "Did you know that God, the one who created you, knows you by name? He cares about you very much. I know it feels lonely when friends and family aren't around, but if you think about how much God cares, it helps. In the meantime, I saw a stack of board games in the closet. How about a little competition?" Mrs. Maxwell added with a wink.

SEASIDE FUN

Find each of the bold words in the word search. Then, write your name on each blank. Read each phrase aloud and think about how important you are to God.

CARES (about) _____   **MADE** _____

LOVES _____   **CALLED** _____

CREATED _____   **SEES** _____

KNOWS _____   **LISTENS (to)** _____

```
L  C  C  R  E  A  T  E  D  Z
B  V  I  L  M  A  D  E  M  G
D  L  G  C  I  G  L  U  L  R
X  I  C  Q  T  V  C  E  R  S
K  S  A  X  X  J  A  Y  K  V
N  T  R  X  H  I  L  L  D  B
O  E  E  S  Y  M  L  O  R  U
W  N  S  I  E  A  E  V  T  U
S  S  W  N  B  E  D  E  F  K
Q  R  M  H  V  S  S  S  F  P
```

Everyone feels alone at times. Talk to God about your feelings and remember that God knows your name and cares about you.

51

So God created man in his own image; he created him in the image of God; he created them male and female.—Genesis 1:27

Olivia stared at her image in the mirror and frowned. Grandma walked by just then and asked, "Why the angry face?"

"My curly hair is driving me crazy," Olivia grumbled. "I can't stand my freckles, and I'd rather be playing football than doing my homework right now!"

Grandma stepped behind Olivia and looked at her in the mirror. "All of us have moments when we are not happy with one thing or the other. But look at that person in the mirror," Grandma said as she pointed at Olivia.

"God made her in His image and believing anything other than that would be believing a lie. You reflect many of His attributes when you are kind, loving, creative, and joyful. God made you just the way you are! He loves your curly hair, your freckles, and your love for football. Give yourself time, Olivia. Some days it will be hard to remember that. But God will help you reflect Him if you trust in His promises."

KITE WORDS

God is so creative! Being made in God's image means we reflect some of God's attributes, or characteristics. List some of those attributes on the kite tail.

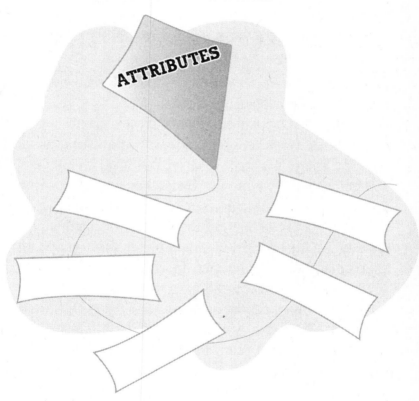

Thank God for making you
just the way He planned.

52

For it was you who created my inward parts; you knit me together in my mother's womb.—Psalm 139:13

Dad, can I ask you something?" Marco asked his dad while they were cleaning the garage.

"Sure, son," Dad replied. "What's on your mind?"

"Well, last week at Bible study we were talking about how God knew us before we were born and how God knit us together inside our moms." Dad looked up at Marco who had stopped cleaning and was sitting still in his wheelchair. "You and Mom have told me about why I was born unable to walk. Did my plan get messed up? Am I less important to God than kids whose bodies are normal?"

Dad walked to Marco and gave him a big hug. "God is perfect and loving, and He knew your story long before you were born. God's love has nothing to do with how hard or easy our lives are. I am sure it is hard to not be able to walk. I don't understand what it's like to be you, and I don't know why God allowed you to go through this hardship. God knows though. Sometimes, in God's love, He allows us to have a hardship because it gives us opportunities to worship Him and share His love in ways we wouldn't be able to otherwise. He planned for your life long before you were born, and He loves every part of you."

SCRIBBLES IN THE SAND

Write the names of the people in your life who love you.
Thank God for each person as you write his or her name.

*Thank God that He planned your
life before you were born!*

53

I will praise you because I have been remarkably and wondrously made. Your works are wondrous, and I know this very well.—Psalm 139:14

Remarkably and *wondrously* are big, impressive words. When David wrote this psalm, he was celebrating the fact that God had made him. He ends the psalm with a phrase that means something like, "And I know that's a fact!"

Most of us have days when we aren't happy with ourselves, but God's Word says we are *wondrous*! Even David, the writer of this psalm, wrote other psalms on days when he was scared, lonely, and grumpy. David had the ability to admit his true feelings to God, write about them, and then focus on God instead of himself. David's psalms often turned to praises the more he thought about God and how much God cared about him.

We can be like David. We can honestly tell God what we're thinking, and then shift our focus to praising Him for making us who we are.

BONFIRE PRAYERS

Fill in the blanks in this prayer starter. Then talk to God about what you wrote. Try this activity on different days when your feelings are different.

Today,
I am feeling . . .

_____

_____

God, You love me no matter what I'm feeling, and that makes me feel . . .

_____

_____

Tell God how you are feeling today, and then thank Him for who He is.

54

"Aren't two sparrows sold for a penny? Yet not one of them falls to the ground without your Father's consent. . . . So don't be afraid; you are worth more than many sparrows."—Matthew 10:29, 31

Jessica sat by the window in her dad's office. Below the window was a bird's nest she had discovered a couple of weeks before. When she first saw the nest, it held three small, blue eggs. Eventually, the baby birds hatched. Today, the birds were about a week old. Jessica named one of the birds Jumper because it moved around more than the others. While she watched, Jumper bounced right out of the nest. "Dad!" Jessica exclaimed. "Jumper fell out of the nest."

Dad got up from his desk and said with a smile, "It's okay; I'll save him." Dad went outside, carefully picked up Jumper, and eased the baby bird into the nest. When Dad came back, he told Jessica, "You can put a baby bird back if the nest is nearby and you are careful. I'm glad you saw Jumper fall! Did you know that God sees everything that happens to you? The Bible says that God knows everything that happens, even to birds." Dad gave Jessica a hug, "And it also says that you are worth more to God than many birds. You are precious to me, too, Jessica."

BEACHCOMBING FINDS

The Bible has several verses that remind us we are important to God and that He cares for us. Look up each reference in your Bible. Circle your favorite verse.

Deuteronomy 31:8

Psalm 55:22

Matthew 6:30

1 Peter 5:7

Matthew 11:28

God says you are worth a lot to Him. Talk to God about how it feels to know He cares.

55

You know when I sit down and when I stand up; you understand my thoughts from far away.—Psalm 139:2

Elliott watched as Aunt Sadie checked her phone. She touched the screen and said, "Rover! Get off the couch!" Aunt Sadie laughed. "I'm training my new dog to stay off the furniture. You should have seen him jump when he heard my voice but thought I wasn't there."

"That would creep me out!" Elliott exclaimed. "I'm glad you don't have a camera on me!"

"I can scold Rover with my voice, but my voice doesn't only scare him. I can also calm him down. It stormed yesterday, and when he heard my voice, he curled up and went to sleep. That reminds me of how God is watching me all the time. If I listen to Him, He warns me when I'm thinking about making a bad decision, and He comforts me when I'm sad."

"I never thought about it that way," Elliott said. "I'm glad God is always watching out for me and even knows what I'm thinking."

SEASIDE FUN

Use the code to solve the message.

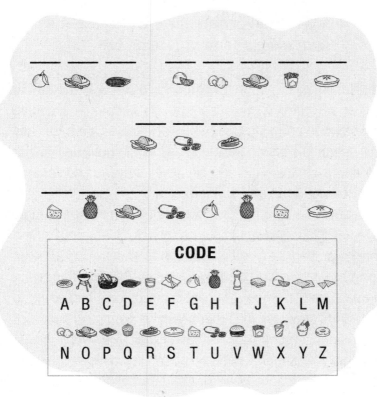

God is looking out for you. Ask God
to help you listen when He nudges
you to do or not do something.

56

"I have loved you with an everlasting love; therefore, I have continued to extend faithful love to you."—Jeremiah 31:3

Jeremiah was a prophet in the Old Testament who had to deliver very difficult messages to his people. The people had stopped honoring God the way He asked them to. They had begun to worship false gods. They did not treat God as the one true God. They did whatever they wanted regardless of what God had told them.

Jeremiah was often sad because he told the people repeatedly that God would punish them for their sins. But the people ignored Jeremiah. God told Jeremiah what He was going to do to Israel. A kingdom called Babylon was going to attack and take over. Many people would be carried off to Babylon to serve the king there. What a sad message!

God encouraged Jeremiah. God knew the people would eventually repent and follow Him. God loved His people and wanted them to love Him. God told Jeremiah that His love was everlasting, and He would continue to show that love to His people.

God cannot allow sin to continue forever. Thankfully, because of God's everlasting love, He provides opportunities for us to ask for forgiveness, turn away from our sins, and follow Him.

KITE WORDS

People sometimes tell us they love us. God says He loves us with *everlasting love*. How is God's love different than a person's love? Write words that describe God's love for us on the kite tail.

EVERLASTING

Is there any sin you need to turn away from? Commit to turning away from sin and following Jesus. Thank God for the everlasting love He has for you.

57

*If we say, "We have no sin,"
we are deceiving ourselves, and the
truth is not in us.—1 John 1:8*

Alex!" Dad called out.

Oh, no, Alex thought. *Dad sounds upset.* Alex leaned his bike against the house and went to the backyard. Alex's dad was standing there, holding a screwdriver and hammer. "Did you use my tools again and not put them back in the garage?" Dad asked sternly.

Alex stammered, "I don't remember. I, um, I think it may have been Lucy. I thought I put them back when I used them."

"Alex," Dad warned. "What's the truth?"

Alex dropped his head and said, "I did it. I really meant to put them away, but I forgot. I'm sorry."

Dad took a deep breath and said, "Thank you for being honest, Alex. If tools are left out in the weather, they can be damaged. But what is worse, when you lie, that is a sin. It's disobeying what God has asked you to do, and that is even more important."

SCRIBBLES IN THE SAND

Think about what happens when you lie or are not truthful.
Write some of your thoughts in the sand below.

*Confessing your sin to God is one part in
receiving forgiveness. Is there something
you need to confess to God today?*

58

*But God proves his own love for us
in that while we were still sinners,
Christ died for us.—Romans 5:8*

Have you ever been punished for something you did? Maybe you didn't finish your homework and lost your phone or computer for a while. Or maybe you were mean to a younger brother or sister and got grounded. But have you ever been punished in place of someone else?

Jesus not only took the punishment for our sins, but He willingly took that punishment before we were even born! Isn't that amazing? The Bible tells us that God knew us before we were ever born, and He also knew that we would sin.

Jesus came to take our punishment. When we confess our sins to Him, we are promised forgiveness. What an amazing thought! God did not respond in anger toward our sin; He acted in love before we were even born.

BONFIRE PRAYERS

Write your thoughts in the prayer starters below.

God,
You knew I would
sin when I . . .

_____

_____

But You love me anyway.
Thank You for . . .

_____

_____

**_Thank God for the amazing gift of forgiveness
we have through Jesus Christ._**

59

But to all who did receive him, he gave them the right to be children of God, to those who believe in his name.—John 1:12

Mrs. Thompson pointed to the poster as the class read John 1:12. Zoey raised her hand and asked, "Aren't we all God's children? We've already studied about how God made the world and all the people."

"That's a great question," Mrs. Thompson replied. "You are right that God made all of us and we are His creation. But do you remember we also learned how people sinned and sin broke our relationship with God?" Zoey nodded, and Mrs. Thompson continued, "Jesus came to take the punishment for our sins. When we ask God to forgive our sins, He does, and that's when we are adopted into God's forever family. We *become* children of God."

"Oh, that makes sense," Zoey said happily. "Trusting in Jesus as my Savior made me a child of God!"

BEACHCOMBING FINDS

Sometimes it's good to dig a little deeper into a Scripture passage. Today's verse is John 1:12. Look up John 1 and read verses 10 through 12. These verses talk about Jesus. Replace every "he" or "him" in verse 12 with "Jesus." Replace every "his" with "Jesus's." Write it out on this page.

John 1:12

_____

_____

_____

_____

_____

Thank God for making it possible for anyone who trusts in Jesus to become a child of God.

60

"Anyone who finds his life will lose it, and anyone who loses his life because of me will find it."—Matthew 10:39

Hey, Granddad," Jake called as he walked to where his granddad was arranging supplies in his tackle box. "Can I ask you something?"

"Of course, you can," Granddad said.

"Last night, you read a verse from the Bible that confused me. It said something about us having to lose our life. That sounded kind of scary," Jake said.

"Oh," Granddad replied. "That doesn't necessarily mean dying. It means to be willing to give up your plans for your life and do what God wants you to do instead."

"Well, I really want to be a counselor when I grow up— just like my dad," Jake said. "Does that mean I should give up that idea?"

"Not necessarily," Granddad explained. "It means you should ask God what He wants you to do first. Sometimes what we want and what God has planned are not the same thing. We just need to care about God's plans for us most."

SEASIDE FUN

It's fun to think about what you might like to do as an adult. Remember to keep praying about it too. Discover some possibilities in the crossword puzzle.

ACROSS

2: A person who makes music
4: A person who teaches a class
5: A person who takes care of money

DOWN

1: A person who helps sick people
2: A person who knows how to fix cars or trucks
3: A person who builds houses

Word Bank: BANKER TEACHER MECHANIC MUSICIAN CARPENTER DOCTOR

It's fun to think about what you want to do when you grow up. Talk to God about it and ask Him to help you know the best plan.

61

A person's heart plans his way,
but the Lord determines his steps.
—Proverbs 16:9

Madison wasn't listening to the show on television, but a commercial got her attention. The lady in the commercial was showing some product that was supposed to be wonderful. Then the lady said, "You control your destiny. Make it great!"

That doesn't sound right to me, Madison thought. She pulled out her journal. She had written some things down after Bible study last week. She found what she was looking for and read the entry aloud: "God is in control. We can make plans, but God is the one who plans our steps. Joy comes when we follow His direction rather than insist on our own way."

Madison closed her journal and thought, *Our teacher was right. People around us may say things that sound true, but it is important to know what God says. I am thankful God is in control. He knows everything, and I don't. I'm glad I can trust Him.*

KITE WORDS

God is in control, but sometimes we forget He is or we don't want Him to be. What things might try to control what you think instead of God? (Here are a couple of ideas: friends, movies, etc.) Write some of your ideas on the kite tail.

Thank God that He is in control of our lives. He knows what's best for us more than we do!

62

For we are his workmanship, created in Christ Jesus for good works, which God prepared ahead of time for us to do.—Ephesians 2:10

Dylan stared at the chore list posted on the refrigerator. His sisters had already picked the chores that sounded easy. He knew he should have looked at the list sooner. "You don't look very happy," Mom said when she saw Dylan standing there.

"I just memorized Ephesians 2:10, but I'm not sure taking out the trash or cleaning the litter box are the good works God planned for me," Dylan said with a sigh.

Mom couldn't help but laugh. "Oh, Dylan. We all have things that we don't like to do. Even our favorite things have not-so-fun parts. I love to paint, but cleaning my brushes afterward is not fun. I have a choice to grumble about cleaning brushes or be thankful for the joy of painting."

Dylan nodded and shrugged. "The pizza boxes in the trash are a reminder of the good food we had last night. And I do love my cat, so I guess these are just the not-so-fun parts of enjoying God's blessings."

"Exactly!" Mom exclaimed. "Now, let's take this trash out together."

SCRIBBLES IN THE SAND

Jot down a list of things you have to do that you don't like to do. What can each of these remind you to be thankful for?

Ask God to help you do your jobs well,
even if some are not so fun.

63

So, whether you eat or drink, or whatever you do, do everything for the glory of God.—1 Corinthians 10:31

Many of the ads you see on social media or hear on television talk about things that make you happy. You may have heard someone say, "Do what makes you happy."

The problem is, even when we think we are happy, that happiness doesn't last long. We soon find ourselves wanting more of what seems to make us happy or wanting something new. One way Satan tempts us is by making us think that just *one more thing* will make us happy.

When we depend on people or things to make us happy, we will eventually feel disappointed. True happiness comes from God. God wants us to change our focus from ourselves to Him. The Bible doesn't say, "Do what makes you happy," but it does say to do "everything for the glory of God." Today's Bible verse reminds us to focus on honoring God while doing even the simplest things, like eating or drinking, and to give God glory for it.

That is the first step to being truly happy in God.

BONFIRE PRAYERS

What is in your hand right now? Thank God for it. Practice doing that today. Keep a list of things you are thankful for.

Ask God to show you how to give
Him glory in all you do.

64

"But the Counselor, the Holy Spirit, whom the Father will send in my name, will teach you all things and remind you of everything I have told you."—John 14:26

You may have learned a lot about God the Father and about Jesus, God the Son. How much have you learned about God the Spirit? The Holy Spirit is the third person of the Trinity; just like Jesus and the Father, He is God!

Jesus promised His disciples that the Holy Spirit would come after He left. When Jesus went back into heaven after His resurrection, the Holy Spirit came to be with believers then, and He is still with us now. The Holy Spirit is called the Counselor. He is the one who helps us recognize God's truth and understand what we need to know when we study the Bible.

You may have had a counselor at camp who watched out for you and gave you good advice about things to do at camp. The Holy Spirit is like our life counselor. He helps us know when we've sinned and need to ask for forgiveness. He helps us have the courage to do the things God wants us to do. He is the one who reminds us of verses from our Bible when we need to be reminded.

BEACHCOMBING FINDS

It's fun to find two halves of a seashell on the beach and put the halves back together. Match each Bible verse reference with its other half, which tells what the verse is about.

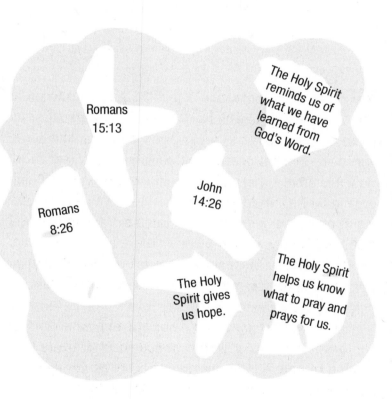

Romans 15:13

The Holy Spirit reminds us of what we have learned from God's Word.

Romans 8:26

John 14:26

The Holy Spirit gives us hope.

The Holy Spirit helps us know what to pray and prays for us.

Thank God for sending the Holy Spirit to be our helper and counselor.

65

As it is written: There is no one righteous, not even one.—Romans 3:10

What kind of homework is that?" Dad asked when he saw Ella at the table with her Bible and the computer.

"It's extra credit," Ella explained. "We get ten points added to our final grade if we can find ten places in the New Testament that use the phrase 'it is written' and explain how it's used."

"That should be interesting," Dad said. "What have you learned so far?"

"Well," Ella began, "so far, they all refer to something written in the Law, the prophets, or psalms—basically parts of our Old Testament. Jesus says it a lot because He quoted the old scriptures. This one I just found in Romans was when Paul was telling them that none of us are good enough to work our way to God. None of us are righteous on our own."

"Great job, Ella!" Dad exclaimed. "You are doing a great job digging into what the Bible says."

SEASIDE FUN

What have you learned so far about each word in the word bank? Do the word search, and ask the Holy Spirit to help you remember what God has taught you.

Word Bank: TRUTH RIGHTEOUS WORD BIBLE HOPE PROMISE WRITTEN FATHER SON SPIRIT

X	K	F	D	W	W	N	N	J	J
T	S	A	P	R	O	M	I	S	E
Q	O	T	T	I	R	R	Q	B	I
S	N	H	Q	T	D	P	R	I	X
Y	D	E	A	T	T	S	P	B	P
P	H	R	Y	E	T	R	O	L	Y
W	O	N	B	N	G	I	U	E	H
L	P	O	S	P	I	R	I	T	X
Y	E	V	N	Q	M	I	K	S	H
R	I	G	H	T	E	O	U	S	Q

Thank God for how the Old and New Testaments support each other. The Bible truly is the Word of God.

66

Listen, my son, and be wise;
keep your mind on the right
course.—Proverbs 23:19

Kai heard his grandpa talking to a neighbor about "what the world makes you think" and how people no longer seemed to know what is true. After the neighbor left, Kai asked his grandpa, "How does the world make you think anything? Isn't the world just this earth we live on?"

Grandpa laughed. He knew what Kai meant. "We do live on this earth, but the people around us are also part of the world. The world, or the people around us, can often make us think things are true that really aren't," Grandpa explained.

"Like what?" Kai asked.

"Well, some people say God is not real. We know that's not true. God is real! We can always test what we hear against God's truth. Do you know where God's truth is found, Kai?"

"The Bible!" Kai exclaimed.

Grandpa smiled, "That's right. We must always compare what we believe to be true to what God says."

KITE WORDS

Who or what in the "world" influences your thoughts? List them on the kite tail. Here are a couple of examples for you: friends, social media, and so on.

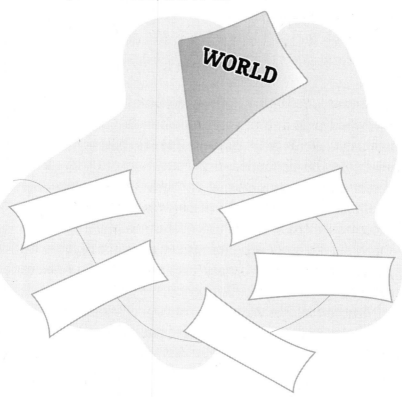

Pray that God will help you recognize what the world says versus what God says so you can keep your mind on the right course.

67

Do not be conformed to this age, but be transformed by the renewing of your mind, so that you may discern what is the good, pleasing, and perfect will of God.—Romans 12:2

One way to study the truth in the Bible is to think about what the words in a verse mean. Romans 12:2 has some interesting words to think about. The first part of the verse says not to be conformed to this age.

Conformed means shaped or molded into a shape, like when you use a bucket to make a sandcastle. The sand becomes the shape of the bucket. This part of the verse is a caution to not become like things in culture just because it's popular. Do your words, actions, or habits look just like people around you who don't follow God, or do they honor God?

Transformed means to experience a change in character or condition. The verse explains that your character can be changed or transformed as you recognize and follow God's perfect will. The verse calls this "the renewing of your mind." You have a fresh outlook when you discover what the good, pleasing, and perfect will of God is.

SCRIBBLES IN THE SAND

Think about the difference between culture (the world) and what honors God. Under "Conform" list things that follow the world's mold. Under "Transform" list things that honor God. (One example is done for you.)

CONFORM

Pretending not to be a
Christian to fit in.

TRANSFORM

Sharing Jesus with my
friends who don't believe.

*Ask God to help you recognize what
is His will and what is simply the
influence of the world around you.*

68

Trust in the Lᴏʀᴅ with all your heart, and do not rely on your own understanding.—Proverbs 3:5

Skylar sat at the table designing a poster like the one she had seen at the mall. She had just finished the lettering for "Follow Your Heart," when Mom walked by and stopped for a look. "What made you choose those words, Skylar?" her mom asked.

"They sounded exciting to me," Skylar explained. "It sounds like doing what makes you happy."

"That can sound like a good thing, but it's easy to choose what we think will make us happy and then make bad choices. That's what happens when we expect people or things to make us happy," Mom said as she hugged Skylar. "God says to trust Him and follow Him. We can do this by reading and knowing the Bible, praying, and asking God to give us hearts that want what He wants. God knows all about us, and He knows our future. When we commit to following God, He directs us along the right paths."

Skylar thought for a moment. "So maybe I should start a new poster and remind myself to trust God first and follow Him!"

BONFIRE PRAYERS

Write a prayer asking God to direct your paths. (You can use words from Proverbs 3:5–6.)

*Ask God to help you trust Him whenever
you are faced with a decision.*

69

Don't be wise in your own eyes;
fear the Lord and turn away
from evil.—Proverbs 3:7

Hey, Dad, I finished my homework. Is it okay if I play video games now?" Miles called out as he went into the den.

"In a minute. Wait for me, I need to fix something." Dad called back.

Miles went into the den and found the two parts of the controller lying on the table. *Oh, I know how to fix this*, Miles thought to himself as he shoved the two pieces together. The two pieces jammed crookedly together, and he realized he had put them on backward.

"I told you to wait just a minute," Dad said sternly as he walked in. "Let me see it. I can fix it."

Miles looked at the floor. "I thought I could fix it," he said.

"It's a lesson we all have to learn. We think we know it all, but we have to learn to do what is right and not rush in when we don't know what we are doing," Dad said calmly.

BEACHCOMBING FINDS

You've just looked at a couple of verses from Proverbs 3. Try doing a little beachcombing to find more truth treasures in Proverbs 3. Write the truth you discover on each message in the bottle.

Proverbs 3:1–2

Proverbs 3:9

Proverbs 3:27

Ask God to help you remember that you don't always know what to do.

70

Now if any of you lacks wisdom, he should ask God—who gives to all generously and ungrudgingly—and it will be given to him.—James 1:5

Angelica carefully followed Nana's instructions as she mixed the cookie dough. Nana explained why they did each step as they worked in the kitchen. "Nana, you are the smartest person in the world!" Angelica exclaimed. "You know everything, don't you?"

Nana laughed as she dried her hands on the kitchen towel. "Oh, my dear, there is so much I don't know. But I don't just want to be smart—I want to have wisdom."

"What is wisdom?" Angelica asked, surprised.

"Wisdom," Nana explained, "is more than just knowing facts. Wisdom means knowing how to make good decisions about what you know. I pray for wisdom every day."

"You do?"

"I do," Nana continued. "James 1:5 says we can ask God for wisdom, and He gives it generously!"

Angelica gave Nana a hug and said, "I'll pray for wisdom too. I want to be like you someday."

SEASIDE FUN

Create the code by numbering the alphabet 1–26. (Example: 1=A, 2=B, 3=C, and so on.) Then use the code to solve for the definition of WISDOM.

___ A	___ H	___ O	___ V
___ B	___ I	___ P	___ W
___ C	___ J	___ Q	___ X
___ D	___ K	___ R	___ Y
___ E	___ L	___ S	___ Z
___ F	___ M	___ T	
___ G	___ N	___ U	

WISDOM IS

___ ___ ___ ___ ___ ___ ___ ___   ___ ___ ___
12 5 1 18 14 9 14 7   8 15 23

___ ___   ___ ___ ___ ___   ___ ___ ___ ___
20 15   12 9 22 5   5 1 3 8

___ ___ ___   ___ ___ ___   ___ ___ ___
4 1 25   9 14 1   23 1 25

___ ___ ___ ___ ___ ___ ___ ___   ___ ___   ___ ___ ___.
16 12 5 1 19 9 14 7   20 15   7 15 4

Thank God for the wisdom
He is generous to give.

71

Guide me in your truth and teach me, for you are the God of my salvation; I wait for you all day long.—Psalm 25:5

Connor and Uncle Dominic had been talking about some things Connor's friends thought were true but weren't. Uncle Dominic knew a lot from the Bible, and Connor liked asking him questions. "Uncle Dom," Connor began, "I don't think it's possible to know the truth about everything!"

"You are right," Uncle Dominic replied.

Connor looked surprised. "I thought you would say to keep studying my Bible, and I would learn all the truth."

"Oh, you'll keep learning, but you'll never learn *all truth*," Uncle Dominic explained. "However, you'll learn what God wants you to know. Do you remember yesterday when you told your little brother something he didn't know? It helped him. That was sharing the truth you have already learned. God guides us through His Word and through other people who have already learned about Him."

KITE WORDS

What do you think it means to "STUDY" your Bible? What tools can you use? Add the ways to study the Bible on the kite tail. Ask an adult about his or her favorite Bible study tool.

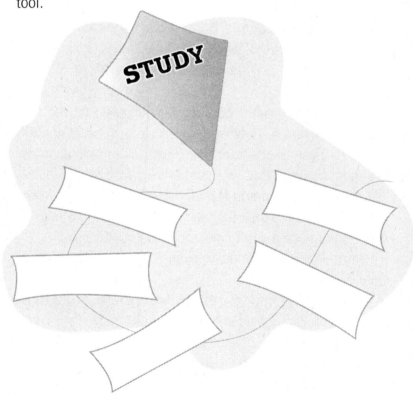

STUDY

Ask God to guide you in His truth and help you continue to learn.

72

*The people here [in Berea] were of more
noble character than those in Thessalonica,
since they received the word with eagerness
and examined the Scriptures daily to see
if these things were so.—Acts 17:11*

Peyton listened to her parents' conversation on the way
home from church. They were talking about something the
pastor had said in the sermon. "Pastor Tim made an interesting comment about what the Bible says about families.
I've never thought about it that way before," Peyton heard
Dad say. "I want to look the passage up and read the verse
in context to see if what he said seems right."

"Dad!" Peyton exclaimed. "Aren't you supposed to believe
what Pastor Tim says?"

"Dad is doing the right thing," Mom explained. "Pastor
Tim often challenges us to double-check what he says with
our Bibles. I'm glad because he is setting a good example for us. God welcomes our questions if we look for the
answers in His Word. Asking questions means we want to
know God's truth."

SCRIBBLES IN THE SAND

Journaling means writing down thoughts. Journal some of your thoughts on this page. What are questions you have for God?

God is never upset with questions. Tell Him things you are curious about.

73

But be doers of the word and not hearers
only, deceiving yourselves.—James 1:22

Nick quickly added the last piece to his model airplane. The whole thing was a bit wobbly, and it suddenly leaned sideways before falling apart. "Oh, no!" Nick yelled. "I can't do this!"

Beau, Nick's older brother, walked into Nick's room. "What's all the yelling about?"

"I'm no good at making models like you are. They just fall apart!" Nick exclaimed angrily.

"Did you follow the instructions? Did you read the part about how to use the glue?" Beau asked.

"Not really. It's just glue. What's the big deal? I needed to be fast," Nick grumbled.

"The instructions are there for a reason. You must read them and then do what they say. When you don't, things don't go the way they should," Beau replied. "It's a lot like what our youth group talked about last night. You can't just read the Bible and then do your own thing. You must do what it says."

BONFIRE PRAYERS

Is there anything the Bible tells you to do that is difficult for you? Write a prayer to God asking Him to help you do what His Word says.

Ask God to help you remember to do what the Bible says and not just read it and forget it.

74

By faith Noah, after he was warned about what was not yet seen and motivated by godly fear, built an ark to deliver his family.—Hebrews 11:7

Chapter 11 of Hebrews is sometimes called "The Hall of Faith." The writer of the book of Hebrews listed several people mentioned in the Old Testament. Each obeyed God by faith. They believed what God had told them even though they did not know the future.

Noah was one of the people mentioned. When Noah was alive, all the people in the world had turned away from God—except for Noah. God planned to destroy everything besides Noah and his family. God told Noah to build an ark, which is a giant boat, so that Noah and his family could be rescued. What do you think it was like for Noah as people watched him build something they had never seen before? Do you think they made fun of him or made him feel silly for building such a big boat? It took over one hundred years, but Noah continued to complete the work God told him to do because he believed God more than he cared about what the people around him thought.

God honored Noah's faithfulness by protecting Noah and his family.

BEACHCOMBING FINDS

Find Hebrews 11 in your Bible and discover some people listed in "The Hall of Faith." Write the person's name by the reference.

Hebrews 11:4

Hebrews 11:7

Hebrews 11:5

Hebrews 11:8

Hebrews 11:20

Hebrews 11:11

Hebrews 11:22

Hebrews 11:23

Hebrews 11:21

Ask God to help you have the courage to obey Him even if those around you don't.

75

For my mouth tells the truth, and wickedness is detestable to my lips.—Proverbs 8:7

Jade waited quietly at the door while Mimi finished typing a sentence on the computer. All the grandkids knew to wait when Mimi was working. At last Mimi looked up. "Hey there, Jade. Thanks for waiting while I finished that thought. What do you need?"

"I told you a lie," Jade began. "I said the dog must have eaten those last two cookies on the plate. But the truth is, I ate them. I've felt so bad since I didn't tell the truth that I finally had to come to tell you."

Mimi nodded knowingly. "I'm proud of you for telling the truth now, Jade. That bad feeling you had is one way the Holy Spirit helps Christians know when they have sinned, and lying is sin. I'm glad you listened and chose to make things right."

Jade went to Mimi for a hug. "I guess we need to make more cookies," Mimi said with a smile.

SEASIDE FUN

Complete the crossword, then use the words to fill in the blanks of the Bible verse.

For my _____ _____ the _____ , and _____ is

_____ to my _____ . (Proverbs 8:7)

Word Bank: WICKEDNESS MOUTH TELLS TRUTH LIPS DETESTABLE

DOWN

1: The part of your face that talks
2: Another word for evil
4: Another word for talks

ACROSS

3: Always tell the _____ .
5: Horrible, revolting
6: These are around your mouth.

Thank God that the Holy Spirit nudges you when you are tempted not to tell the truth.

76

Love finds no joy in unrighteousness but rejoices in the truth.—1 Corinthians 13:6

Xavier was riding home from vacation with his Aunt Cate and Uncle Bill. Xavier was playing his video game in the back seat, but he could hear his aunt and uncle talking. Aunt Cate was telling Uncle Bill that his teasing might have hurt their mamaw's feelings during lunch.

Xavier couldn't hear everything they said, but Uncle Bill didn't get angry. Later, Xavier asked his uncle about the conversation: "Did Aunt Cate make you mad?"

Uncle Bill winked at Xavier, "Well, I may have felt irritated inside at first. But Aunt Cate was kind when she told me, and mostly, I was sad that I had hurt Mamaw's feelings. I know Aunt Cate loves me, so I appreciate it when she tells me the truth. It can help me make better choices."

KITE WORDS

Today's Bible verse says that love rejoices in the truth. What does the word *rejoice* mean to you? Write some similar words on the kite tail.

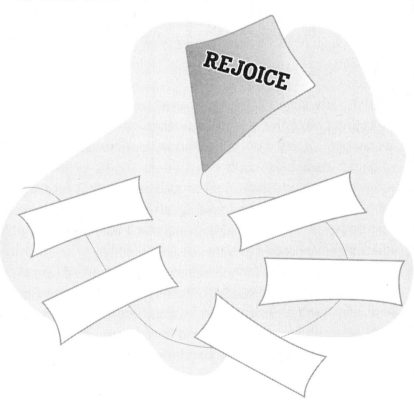

***Ask God for the people who love you
enough to tell you the truth.***

77

But speaking the truth in love, let us grow in every way into him who is the head—Christ.—Ephesians 4:15

Aha!" Madeline exclaimed as she pointed her finger at a verse in the Bible. "Gracie is wrong! And I just found the verse to prove it. I can't wait to show her. She won't feel so big and important then!"

Madeline and Gracie had argued earlier that morning about whether the Bible says Jonah was swallowed by a big fish or a whale, and Madeline was thrilled when she discovered she was right. It was a big fish!

Mrs. Owen heard Madeline and commented, "I'm proud of you for going to the Bible to be sure about the truth. But knowing the truth is only part of what God asks of us. He also tells us to speak the truth in love. We're not trying to make someone feel wrong or embarrassed. That can make them feel angry, and then they usually don't listen to what we have to say."

Madeline looked back down at her Bible. "Gracie was so hateful to me, I wanted to be hateful back—especially when I knew I was right."

"Let's pray for Gracie first, and we'll also pray that God will help you speak the truth in love to Gracie," Mrs. Owen said.

SCRIBBLES IN THE SAND

How can you prepare to speak the truth in love if you are upset? List some ideas in the sand. One idea has been written to help you get started.

- Walk away and think about how to speak kindly in a loving way.

-

-

-

-

Ask God to help you speak the truth in love, just as Jesus did.

78

For I am not ashamed of the gospel, because it is the power of God for salvation to everyone who believes, first to the Jew, and also to the Greek.—Romans 1:16

Theo gathered his ball and glove to play catch with his new neighbor. He walked by his dad on the way out. "Where are you heading?" Dad asked, looking up from the computer.

"I'm going to play catch with the new kid next door. They just moved in. We are hitting it off," Theo paused. "Their family does a lot of things differently than we do. It's been fun to try their foods and learn their games. But their religion doesn't worship the same God we do. It's okay to still be friends, right?"

"Absolutely!" Dad declared. "And it's okay to tell them about the God you worship. When you do, just remember how much God loves you and what Jesus did for all of us. When you think about God's love first, people will hear that love in your voice when you talk. Don't be ashamed of what you believe. Trust God to help you share your faith with others. He promised He would."

"Thanks, Dad," Theo said. "I like my new friend. I'm excited to get to know him more and tell him about Jesus."

BONFIRE PRAYERS

Do you know people who don't know about Jesus or how much He loves them? Pray that they will learn how much Jesus loves them. List their names here as a prayer list you can pray for every day.

Ask God to help you not be ashamed to talk about Jesus with your friends. Ask Him to help you show love when you tell others about Him.

79

Therefore, if anyone is in Christ, he is a new creation; the old has passed away, and see, the new has come!—2 Corinthians 5:17

Claire stormed onto the patio and flopped into the swing with her arms folded. Aunt Camila was enjoying a glass of lemonade in the sun. She noticed the look on Claire's face. "I'm guessing you are angry about something," Aunt Camila observed.

"James gets on my last nerve!" Claire huffed about her little brother, then sighed. "I get so mad; I just need to walk away or get outside for a while."

Aunt Camila nodded, "I know exactly what you mean. Your dad is my little brother, and I have a terrible temper—I get mad easily too."

Claire looked surprised. "You are the calmest person I know! I can't remember ever seeing you get angry."

"It used to be a real problem," Aunt Camila admitted, "and I still struggle with it, but my temper is one of the things God has been helping me change since I became a Christian. I love God's promise that He makes us a new creation. He is always changing my heart to make it more like Jesus's."

BEACHCOMBING FINDS

Today's verse, 2 Corinthians 5:17, helps us know how God is changing us for His good. Philippians 1:6 also helps us discover a great truth about God's work in our lives.

Locate Philippians 1:6 in your Bible, and then fill in the blanks where the waves have washed away some words.

I am _____ of this,

that he who _____ a _____

_____ in you

will carry it to completion until the day of

_____ _____. (Philippians 1:6)

God can change us when we trust Him. Ask God to help you trust Him as you become more like Jesus.

80

Therefore, be imitators of God, as dearly loved children.—Ephesians 5:1

Santiago swaggered into the kitchen and climbed onto the kitchen stool. Papaw placed a bowl of cereal in front of Santiago, then raised his eyebrows in surprise. "Where did you get that outfit? I think you have some of it on backward."

"No, Papaw," Santiago said as he sat up straighter. "This is what all my friends decided to wear today. It's what our favorite singer wears."

Papaw thought for a moment, then said, "Imitating what a singer or movie hero wears can be fun. But whose actions are you imitating?"

"What do you mean?" Santiago asked.

"The Bible tells Christians to imitate Jesus because we are His dearly loved children. You can dress like your friends, but your actions should show that you follow Jesus," Papaw replied.

SEASIDE FUN

What types of people are often imitated? Find the words in the word search, and then highlight the one you should imitate.

Word Bank: ACTOR ACTRESS SINGER ATHLETE FAMOUS WEALTHY POLITICIAN JESUS

I	L	C	K	B	K	K	P	J	N
A	C	T	R	E	S	S	O	X	F
T	T	F	O	Z	I	M	L	W	A
S	V	H	B	F	U	D	I	E	M
F	I	L	L	D	A	S	T	A	O
A	J	N	M	E	C	M	I	L	U
U	E	Y	G	J	T	Y	C	T	S
H	S	J	A	E	O	E	I	H	Q
D	U	W	L	H	R	I	A	Y	M
T	S	K	C	X	P	B	N	J	W

Ask God to help you imitate
Jesus's actions every day.

81

Dear friends, do not believe every spirit, but test the spirits to see if they are from God, because many false prophets have gone out into the world.—1 John 4:1

How was Ms. Eleanor doing?" Mom asked as Nora came in the back door after taking her neighbor some freshly baked muffins.

"She was doing good today," Nora said. "She was excited about the muffins. She didn't talk much because she was watching a preacher on television. Mom, I heard the preacher promise things to the people watching if they would send him money. He even made the promise that people like Ms. Eleanor could be healed from their sicknesses. Ms. Eleanor said she wished she had money to send him. Do you think he was telling the truth?"

"I don't, Nora. The Bible warns us that sometimes people will claim they speak for God, but if something doesn't sound right, ask questions and check what the Bible says," Mom explained. "Maybe next time we go to Ms. Eleanor's house, we can ask her if she wants to read the Bible together."

"Good idea, Mom. Next time, I'll try to go when her show isn't on so we can talk more," Nora said thoughtfully. "I want her to know we care about her, and God loves her, even if she doesn't have money to send to a pastor."

KITE WORDS

In the Bible, a prophet was someone who proclaimed God's message.

Today, pastors or preachers proclaim God's message by talking about how God's Word applies to us. What are some other words that mean PROCLAIM? Write them on the kite tail.

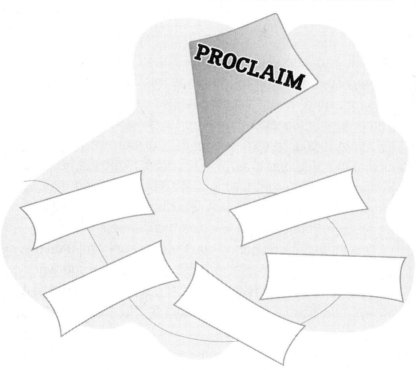

Ask God to help you recognize whether what someone says is true to God's Word or not.

82

*Do not be surprised, brothers and sisters,
if the world hates you.—1 John 3:13*

Josiah had attended the same school since he was in kindergarten. Then, in fourth grade, his family moved to a different state. Many things changed, including the local school he started attending. The teachers were nice, and he made a couple of new friends, but not everyone was nice to him. A group of guys in his class found out he went to church and started calling him "Bible Guy" and making fun of him. No one in his last school had made fun of him for being a Christian. So why was this happening now?

One night Josiah opened his devotion book and read the Bible verse for the day: "Do not be surprised if the world hates you." Josiah *was* surprised. "I guess Christians have always had people who were mean to them just because they believed in Jesus."

Josiah decided not to be mean back. Instead, he prayed for them and tried not to let their insults bother him. He also prayed to make new friends who believed in Jesus as he did.

SCRIBBLES IN THE SAND

It's time to journal. Write about a time you should have been nicer to someone when he or she was mean to you. Pray for them and remember how much God loves you.

Thank God that He loves you even if others treat you hatefully. Ask God to help you remember that He loves them too.

83

Love one another deeply as brothers and sisters. Take the lead in honoring one another.—Romans 12:10

Leilani tossed her vest on the couch. "Hey, aren't you going to show me your new badges?" Nanny asked. "You have worked so hard, and I'm proud of you. Weren't you getting two new badges for your vest tonight?"

"Who cares!" Leilani grumbled. "Paisley earned four! I'll never have as many as she does. Just once I'd like to be the best at something."

Nanny picked up the vest and looked at the badges. "These badges are proof you worked very hard. I am so proud of you. But I know a badge of honor that is even more important than the ones on your vest."

Leilani was surprised. "What badge is that?"

"Well, it's not one you sew on a vest. It's when you honor God with your actions even when you don't win an award. God tells us to take the lead in honoring one another. When we do that, we also honor Him. That is the biggest honor of all."

BONFIRE PRAYERS

Ask God to help you think of friends you can encourage.
Write a prayer asking God to be with each of those friends.

*Do you wish you could do something someone
else does well? Try praying for that person. Ask
God to help you honor and encourage them.*

84

Adopt the same attitude as that of
Christ Jesus.—Philippians 2:5

Ryan looked at the list of Bible verses he was memorizing for his Bible club at church. They earned awards every time they memorized ten verses. They also got stars if they could explain the verses. "Grandma," Ryan said. "I'm supposed to explain a Bible verse, but I'm not sure what it means. What does it mean to 'adopt the same attitude' as Jesus?"

"Well, let's think about what we know about Jesus," Grandma began. "How did He treat people?"

"He was kind to people in need," Ryan said thoughtfully. "He taught His followers important things about God. And He was patient."

"That's all right. He also never shied away from the truth. He always told people that they needed to repent from sin and turn to God, but He did that with wisdom and kindness," Grandma remarked.

"Oh, I get it!" exclaimed Ryan. "We need to think about how Jesus acted in different situations and choose that same attitude."

"I knew you'd think it through!" praised Grandma. "Great job, Ryan."

BEACHCOMBING FINDS

Philippians 2:5 is today's Bible verse. It is the beginning of a group of verses that tell important things about Jesus. See what treasures you can dig up by reading and thinking about each verse. List one treasure or piece of information about Jesus that you find in each verse.

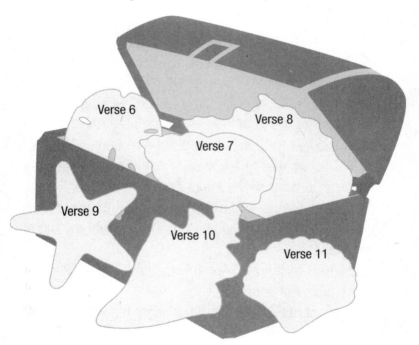

Verse 6

Verse 8

Verse 7

Verse 9

Verse 10

Verse 11

Ask God to help you remember to choose the attitude Jesus demonstrated when He was with other people.

85

A contrary person spreads conflict, and a gossip separates close friends.—Proverbs 16:28

Piper and Autumn were practicing soccer kicks in Piper's backyard. "You will never believe what I heard about Coach Angie!" Autumn exclaimed. "I'm not sure whether it's true or not, but a lot of the girls were talking about her."

Piper thought for a minute while she picked up the soccer ball. She wanted to know what Autumn knew, but she had recently been learning about gossip. "That's okay," she finally said. "I'd rather you didn't tell me. I don't want to talk about Coach Angie, especially if the things we say might not be true."

"But what can it hurt?" Autumn asked. "She would never know we talked about her."

"She might not. But if she did, it might hurt her feelings, and I wouldn't want to do that." Piper explained. "So if it's okay with you, I'd rather keep practicing our soccer kicks. Are you ready? It's your turn."

Autumn shrugged her shoulders and lined up for her kick.

SEASIDE FUN

Today's Bible verse talked about gossip. What does *gossip* mean? Solve for the definition by writing the letter in the blank that comes after the letter below the blank. Two of them have been done for you.

Gossip means

S A Y I N G   T H I N G S
R Z X H M F   S G H M F R

A B O U T   A P E R S O N
Z A N T S   Z O D Q R N M

T H A T   M A Y   N O T
S G Z S   L Z X   M N S

B E   T R U E.
A D   S Q T D.

It can be tempting to listen when someone wants to talk about another person. Ask God to help you not be a part of gossip.

86

Not neglecting to gather together, as some are in the habit of doing, but encouraging each other, and all the more as you see the day approaching.—Hebrews 10:25

Are we picking up your friend Luka for church this morning?" Dad asked as he and Ryder climbed into the SUV.

"I don't think so," Ryder said sadly. "He usually calls to say if he's going or not. His family was out late last night at some family picnic. He said he might be too tired this morning."

"Why don't you give him a quick call?" Dad pulled his cell phone out and handed it to Ryder. "Maybe he just needs some encouragement. If he knows you are hoping he'll come, it might give him the nudge he needs."

Ryder was excited when he hung up from talking to Luka. "He said he's coming!" Ryder exclaimed. "He thought it was too late to call. He'll be ready when we get there."

"Let's go." Dad said with a smile.

KITE WORDS

Today's Bible verse mentioned encouraging each other. What are ways you can encourage your friends? Write your thoughts on the kite tail.

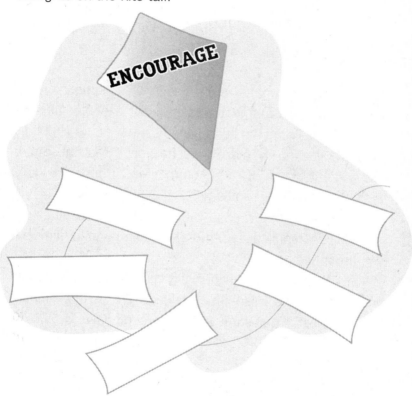

Ask God to help you want to gather with friends at church. Pray for friends who don't come often and ask God to give you opportunities to invite them.

87

*For you are saved by grace through faith,
and this is not from yourselves; it is
God's gift—not from works, so that no
one can boast.—Ephesians 2:8–9*

Sophia and Hannah were working on a school project together. The assignment was to make a poster about a poem. Sophia read the poem aloud so they could plan their artwork. The poem mentioned heaven. "Heaven sounds like a great place," Sophia commented. "I hope I'm good enough to go there someday."

"It's not about how good you are," Hannah replied.

"What?" Sophia asked. "Surely you can't go to heaven if you are a bad person."

"The Bible says that technically, everyone is a bad person according to God," Hannah explained. "We have all sinned, and we deserve punishment. But the good news is …"

Sophia cut her off. "You're telling me that no one can get to heaven?"

"Not at all! The Bible also says that when anyone—even the worst person—believes in Jesus and repents from sin, they can be forgiven," Hannah explained.

"Really?" Sophia said puzzled. "I don't know that I understand. Can you tell me more about Jesus and how this forgiveness works?"

Hannah smiled, "I would love to!"

SCRIBBLES IN THE SAND

How would you answer a friend who says he or she hopes to be good enough to go to heaven? Write your answer in the sand.

Thank God for His gift of forgiveness and salvation through Jesus.

88

Sitting down, he [Jesus] called the Twelve and said to them, "If anyone wants to be first, he must be last and servant of all."—Mark 9:35

Leonardo was so excited about the end-of-season baseball banquet. Not only had his team won the championship, but his cousin Brooks was also going to be the guest speaker. Brooks had just signed with a major league baseball team.

"Hey, Brooks!" Leonardo called when he saw his cousin. "Let's go sit over here," Leonardo said. Just as he turned, he ran headfirst into a server carrying a tray of rolls that showered down everywhere. Leonardo was then horrified when he saw Brooks on his hands and knees helping the server gather up all the rolls.

Later, Leonardo apologized for the mishap. "I'm so sorry. You were the guest of honor, and you shouldn't have been the one on the floor picking up all those rolls."

"Leo," Brooks said. "Jesus teaches us to serve others. I care a lot more about honoring Him than being honored by others. I hope that was the most important thing I taught you and your team today."

BONFIRE PRAYERS

Confession is an important part of praying. Write a prayer to God telling Him some ways you forget to put others first.

Ask God to help you worry less about looking important and focus more on helping others.

89

Do nothing out of selfish ambition or conceit, but in humility consider others as more important than yourselves.—Philippians 2:3

Dad and I decided that you and your sister may each bring a friend along on our camping trip next week. Doesn't that sound fun?" Mom asked Riley.

Riley was thrilled. "It does!" Riley thought for a moment, and then said, "Maybe I should invite Anna. She is popular, and I want to get invited to her parties."

"Oh," Mom said thoughtfully. "What about your friend Cora? You seemed to have so much fun together when she came over last week."

"Well, Mom," Riley began, "Cora doesn't have a lot of friends. I like her, but I want to be a part of the popular group."

"It's okay if you and Anna have fun together and you want to invite her because you want to spend time with her, but I want you to think about something. When we try to make ourselves look good or important, the Bible calls that conceit or selfish ambition," Mom explained. "When we value ourselves more than other people, that doesn't honor God."

Riley thought about it for a while, then came back to her mom. "You're right," Riley said. "I was just thinking about myself. Cora and I have lots of fun together. I'll ask her."

BEACHCOMBING FINDS

First Corinthians 13 says a lot about agape love, which is the kind of love that puts others first.

Look up 1 Corinthians 13:4–7 and write one phrase that describes love on each of the treasures you find on the beach.

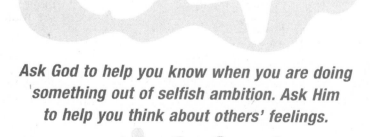

Ask God to help you know when you are doing something out of selfish ambition. Ask Him to help you think about others' feelings.

90

Therefore, whatever you want others to do for you, do also the same for them, for this is the Law and the Prophets.—Matthew 7:12

Carson marched into the kitchen and grabbed a black marker from the pencil cup. "What are you going to do with that?" his older brother, Jase, asked.

"Emmett drives me crazy!" Carson shouted. He was so mad at their little brother. "He drew all over my school project, so I'm going to scribble on his precious dinosaur!"

"Hold on, Carson," Jase warned. "What Emmett did was wrong. But think about the consequences if you damage his favorite toy. And besides that, you're older than he is. He is still learning how to respect other people's things."

Carson's shoulders slumped. "You're right. I'd get into trouble and my project would still be messed up."

"That's right. And this way, you can treat Emmett the way you would want to be treated. Listen," Jase said putting aside his book, "show me your project. Maybe I can help you fix it. I seem to remember you doing the same thing to one of my assignments. I may have some experience at repairing homework."

SEASIDE FUN

Find words from today's Bible verse in the word search, then try saying Matthew 7:12 by only looking at the words in the word bank.

Word Bank: WHATEVER WANT OTHERS YOU ALSO SAME THEM LAW PROPHETS

A	W	I	O	O	S	Q	F	L	M
K	U	H	C	T	R	U	S	A	W
P	M	M	A	T	H	E	M	Y	T
J	R	H	M	T	Y	E	D	O	D
W	K	O	B	S	E	H	R	U	L
X	A	G	P	N	A	V	U	S	A
A	X	N	X	H	G	M	E	C	W
L	Q	M	T	O	E	M	E	R	L
S	T	Z	N	G	P	T	B	D	B
O	Y	U	W	Y	D	I	S	D	D

Ask God to help you treat others the way you want to be treated rather than trying to get back at them when you are angry.

91

Do not be deceived: "Bad company corrupts good morals."—1 Corinthians 15:33

Ember climbed into the car when her aunt picked her up from school. "So, you had to stay after school today, huh?" Aunt Suzie asked. "Mom asked me to pick you up since she had to work."

Ember leaned back in the seat. "It wasn't even my fault!" she declared. "Josie was the one who broke the rules. I just happened to be there too."

"'Bad company corrupts good morals,'" Aunt Suzie said as she pulled the car into traffic.

"What does that mean?" Ember asked.

"It means when you spend time with people who are doing things they shouldn't, you can begin to pick up their habits," explained Aunt Suzie.

"But I thought we were supposed to be friends with everyone. Isn't that in the Bible too?" Ember retorted.

"You're right. It is," Aunt Suzie agreed. "But the Bible also helps us know how to be friends. Don't follow the bad choices your friends make. Stick up for what you believe and search out friends who feel the same way. I hope you can learn to be a good friend to Josie, but you either need to stand up for what's right or walk away if she is about to break the rules next time."

KITE WORDS

Morals are the behaviors you value. What are some examples of good morals? Write them on the kite tail.

Ask God to help you recognize the difference between good and bad choices.

92

Don't worry about anything, but in everything, through prayer and petition with thanksgiving, present your requests to God. And the peace of God, which surpasses all understanding, will guard your hearts and minds in Christ Jesus.—Philippians 4:6–7

Most people worry about things now and then.

Worry means thinking about what might happen so much that you feel anxious or concerned. It is a normal human feeling. But God tells us what to do instead of worrying.

Prayer is talking to God. We can tell Him what is bothering us, and we can ask Him to help in every situation. The Bible says to thank Him for being in control, even before He answers our prayer. Talking to God, asking for His help, and thanking Him for being in control are all part of trusting God. When we trust God, we can feel peace, which is often hard for people around us to understand. Trusting God doesn't mean that the things we worry about won't happen, but we know God is with us and He is in control. The truth is, many of the things we worry about never happen.

No matter what, God is with us, and He loves us more than we can imagine.

SCRIBBLES IN THE SAND

Journal time. What are some things you tend to worry about? Write them in the sand, and then pray about them.

Are you worried about something now? Tell God and thank Him for being in control.

93

No temptation has come upon you except what is common to humanity. But God is faithful; he will not allow you to be tempted beyond what you are able, but with the temptation he will also provide the way out so that you may be able to bear it.—1 Corinthians 10:13

Mrs. Cranford read 1 Corinthians 10:13 aloud to the Bible study class. "So," Mrs. Cranford commented, "how do you think God provides ways of escape from our temptations?"

The kids were quiet for a while. Then Austin timidly replied, "Well, like when I see answers on someone else's test, I can look the other way."

"Or if you see money at home that isn't yours, you can tell your mom instead of taking it," added Nicole.

"Maybe even remembering that God is always seeing you even when people aren't," chimed in Brody.

"All of those are great answers!" declared Mrs. Cranford. "Sometimes you just have to look for those ways of escape, because they are always there. God promises they will be."

BONFIRE PRAYERS

How would you complete these prayer sentences?

God,
when I am tempted
to lie to my parents, help me . . .

_____

_____

When I am tempted to take something that
doesn't belong to me, help me . . .

_____

_____

When I feel angry with my best friend, help me . . .

_____

_____

*Ask God to help you recognize how to avoid
temptation the next time you are faced with it.*

94

*My brothers and sisters, do not show
favoritism as you hold on to the faith in our
glorious Lord Jesus Christ.—James 2:1*

Luis and Enzo met at the local skate park almost every Saturday. Enzo often talked to his friend about Jesus, and Luis asked lots of questions. Enzo was so excited the day Luis called to say he had trusted in Jesus as his Savior.

One Saturday when they met at the park, Luis told Enzo, "I'm being baptized tomorrow! Can you come? I know our church isn't as nice or fancy as yours, but I really would like for you to be there."

"That sounds great! I want to come. I'll ask Mom to bring me!" Enzo exclaimed. "I know our churches are different, but that doesn't matter. Now we are brothers!"

"We are?" Luis asked.

"Yes, we are," Enzo assured him. "God does not show favoritism, and He says neither should we. Salvation is for all who believe, and believers are brothers and sisters in Christ. Welcome to the family!" Enzo exclaimed, giving Luis a high five.

BEACHCOMBING FINDS

Digging deeper into a section of Scripture is like digging for treasure along the beach. Follow the instructions below to dig deeper about what God's Word is teaching.

Locate and read James 2:1–9 in your Bible.

What is this passage teaching?

_____

_____

_____

_____

Describe a situation like the one in verses 2–4 that you might experience.

_____

_____

_____

_____

Ask God to help you share the gospel with everyone around you and not to show favoritism.

95

And not only that, but we also boast in our afflictions, because we know that affliction produces endurance, endurance produces proven character, and proven character produces hope.—Romans 5:3–4

Rose helped put a pillow under her mom's leg. Her mom had broken her leg in a car accident last week. Mom was in a lot of pain, and their car was in the shop. "Thanks, sweetie," Mom said. "That helps. I'm sorry we didn't get to leave for Grandma's today as we had hoped, but God has been faithful, and He'll give us what we need."

"Do you believe that after the things that happened? I thought the Bible said to ask for whatever we want, and God gives it. Why does God let bad things happen?" Rose asked.

"The Bible does say that, but it says more too. You can't just pick a verse and stop there," Mom cautioned. "That's how people begin to believe things that aren't true. God does tell us to ask for what we want, but the Bible also tells us that things won't always go the way we want. We live in a broken world where accidents, illness, and other things happen. Sometimes God protects us from them, and sometimes He helps us through them. But God promises that even when we go through hard times or afflictions, He makes us more like Jesus. I want to learn how to trust Him when anything comes along—good or bad."

SEASIDE FUN

Sometimes it helps to look up the definitions of words to understand what a Bible verse says. Use words from today's verse to fill in the crossword puzzle. The clues are the definitions of the words.

ACROSS
1: Attributes or qualities of a person (like good or dependable)
5: Shown to be worthy or capable
6: Talk or be happy about

DOWN
2: Causes of suffering or difficulties
3: The ability to withstand hardship or suffering
4: Confident expectation

Word Bank: ENDURANCE HOPE BOAST AFFLICTIONS CHARACTER PROVEN

Thank God that He uses even difficult times to help you grow in character and hope.

96

"If I go away and prepare a place for you, I will come again and take you to myself, so that where I am you may be also."—John 14:3

Grant and his family went to the memorial service for their neighbor, Mrs. Weeks. She was an elderly lady who had recently died. "That was the first memorial service you've ever been to," said Mom. "If you want to ask any questions, it's okay."

"Well," Grant began, "I liked when people talked about the nice things she did. She was always nice to us and even remembered our birthdays. I know she loved Jesus, and it was good to hear the pastor talk about her being in heaven with Jesus. But I do have a question."

"What's that?" Mom encouraged.

"I heard some people in the seats behind us whispering," Grant explained. "One of them said he hoped there was a heaven, but he doubted it. Heaven is real, isn't it?"

"Jesus Himself promised that heaven is real," Mom assured Grant. "The Bible promises that when anyone who trusts in Jesus as Savior dies, they are instantly with Jesus. I will miss Mrs. Weeks, but I know I'll see her again."

"Whew, that's a relief," Grant sighed. "I'm glad we can read the Bible and know for sure heaven is real."

KITE WORDS

The Bible tells us that Christians will live forever in God's presence. There will be no more disease or death. We will be with Jesus and reunited with people we loved who were also believers. List on the kite tail a few things that you are glad to know about heaven.

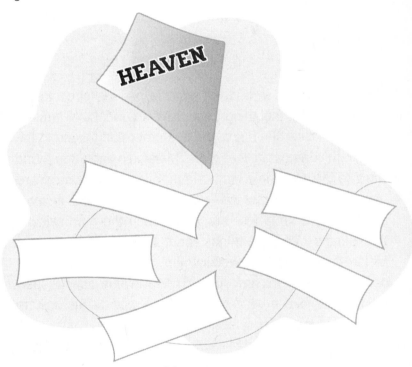

Thank Jesus that His eternal plans include preparing heaven for those who trust in Him.

97

"You are a king then?" Pilate asked. "You say that I'm a king," Jesus replied. "I was born for this, and I have come into the world for this: to testify to the truth. Everyone who is of the truth listens to my voice." "What is truth?" said Pilate.—John 18:37–38

Melanie turned to a clean page in her sketchbook and began to draw the things she saw around their family's campsite. While she drew, she heard her dad talking to the man in the camper next to them. Melanie's dad often found ways to talk to people he met about Jesus. Melanie heard her dad talk about Jesus in a very friendly and encouraging way. Melanie was surprised when the man said he didn't know if all those things about Jesus were true or not. Melanie's dad finished helping the man and then walked back over to their campsite. "Dad," Melanie asked, "that man seems like a very smart person, but did he say he didn't believe in Jesus?"

"That's what he said," Dad replied sadly. "We shouldn't be surprised or upset if someone who seems important or smart doesn't believe what we know the Bible says is true. Jesus faced the same thing. The Bible doesn't tell us to convince people. It only says to share what we know. And we can pray for people like our fellow campers."

SCRIBBLES IN THE SAND

What are some truths you know about Jesus? Write them in the sand below.

Ask God to help you know the truth and to share that truth with others.

98

For the time will come when people will not tolerate sound doctrine, but according to their own desires, will multiply teachers for themselves because they have an itch to hear what they want to hear. They will turn away from hearing the truth and will turn aside to myths.—2 Timothy 4:3–4

Bookstore day was one of Andrew's favorite days during school break. Aunt Libby took Andrew and his two cousins to the bookstore to pick out new books. Andrew found Aunt Libby in the religion section. "What are you looking at, Aunt Libby?"

"It's a new Bible study about Psalms," Aunt Libby said, showing him the book.

"There are a lot of books in this section!" Andrew exclaimed. "How do you know which ones to read?"

Aunt Libby replied, "Sometimes authors twist what the Bible says to teach what they want to teach. I only pick authors I know can be trusted to stick with God's truth. I have to look a little harder and read a little more, but it's always worth it."

Andrew was surprised. "I thought if someone was an adult and had written a book, it must be true."

"Not necessarily," Aunt Libby explained. "That's why we always pay attention to who is writing it and what they believe."

BONFIRE PRAYERS

Write a prayer for the Bible teachers in your life. Pray that God will guide them as they teach you and your friends.

Ask God to help you read His Word and know what it says rather than just listening to people who teach the things you want to hear.

99

Then we will no longer be little children, tossed by the waves and blown around by every wind of teaching, by human cunning with cleverness in the techniques of deceit.—Ephesians 4:14

Can you think of things you know or can do today that you couldn't do five years ago? You've grown a lot, and you know so much more than you did then.

Imagine how much more you will grow and learn in another five years! Today's Bible verse reminds us how important it is to grow in our faith. If we don't, we can easily believe anything we hear. That's what "tossed by the waves and blown around by every wind of teaching" means. We can grow in our faith by reading the Bible and knowing what it says, listening to wisdom from older Christians, and praying and asking God to help us grow.

Sometimes people can be very convincing, even if what they teach goes against what God says in His Word. Sometimes people might even make you think that some truths in the Bible are wrong. God's Word is always true. The more you read and study God's Word, both alone and with other Christians, the stronger your faith will grow. When you grow spiritually, you are better equipped to stand against the winds and waves of false teaching.

BEACHCOMBING FINDS

Locate each of the Bible verses listed on the seashells. Then, answer the question on the driftwood.

John 15:26

1 Corinthians 2:10

John 14:26

2 Peter 1:21

What promise is in all these verses? Who will help you know, understand, and remember God's Word?

_____

_____

_____

_____

Commit to God that you will continue to read His Word and learn the things the Holy Spirit will teach you.

100

"You will know the truth, and the truth will set you free."—John 8:32

Some people have a hard time believing in Jesus. Even many of the religious leaders of Jesus's day did not believe Jesus was the one God promised to send as Savior. Today's Bible verse is part of a conversation Jesus had with some people one day.

Jesus explained to the people that when someone sins, that person is a *slave* to sin. Sin is doing what we want to do even when God says it is wrong. *Slave* can be a scary word. It means that sin is the master of that person's life. But Jesus also said that when we follow Him, we are His disciples. Following Jesus means we spend time with Jesus, trust Him, and try to be more like Him every day. Jesus said that knowing the truth is what sets us free. The truth is, we are all sinners, and our sin deserves to be punished; however, God loves us and sent His Son Jesus takes the punishment for our sins so that we can have forgiveness if we will repent, or turn away, from our sins and follow Jesus. That is the most important truth in the world.

The truth always points us to Jesus.

SEASIDE FUN

God's truth is truth in any language! Use the sign language chart to solve the code and discover one more important truth.

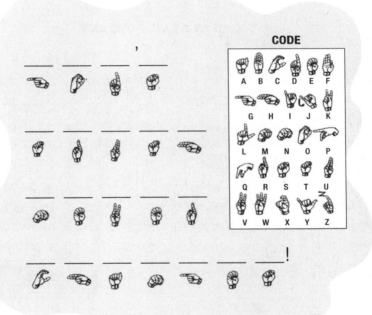

CODE

Thank God for the truth found in His Word that truly sets you free.

WORD SEARCH PUZZLES

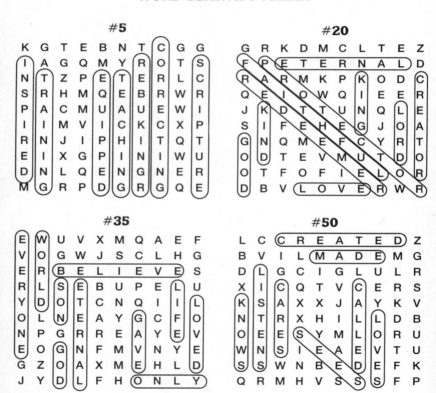

#5

```
K  G  T  E  B  N  T  C  G  G
I  A  G  Q  M  Y  R  O  T  S
N  T  Z  P  E  T  E  R  L  C
S  R  H  C  M  Q  B  R  W  R
P  A  C  M  U  E  U  E  W  I
I  I  M  V  I  A  K  C  X  P
R  N  J  I  P  C  I  T  Q  T
E  I  X  G  P  H  N  I  W  U
D  N  L  Q  E  I  G  N  E  R
M  G  R  P  D  N  G  R  G  E
```

#20

```
G  R  K  D  M  C  L  T  E  Z
F  P  E  T  E  R  N  A  L  D
R  A  R  M  K  P  K  O  D  C
Q  E  I  O  W  Q  I  E  E  R
J  K  D  T  T  U  N  G  L  E
S  I  F  E  H  E  G  J  O  A
G  N  Q  M  E  F  C  Y  R  T
O  D  T  E  V  M  U  T  D  O
O  T  F  O  F  I  E  L  O  R
D  B  V  L  O  V  E  R  W  R
```

#35

```
E  W  U  V  X  M  Q  A  E  F
V  O  G  W  J  S  C  L  H  G
E  R  B  E  L  I  E  V  E  S
R  L  S  E  B  U  P  E  L  U
Y  D  O  T  C  N  Q  I  I  L
O  L  N  E  A  Y  G  C  F  O
N  P  G  R  R  E  A  Y  E  V
E  O  G  N  F  M  V  N  Y  E
G  Z  Y  A  X  M  E  H  L  D
J  Y  D  L  F  H  O  N  L  Y
```

#50

```
L  C  C  R  E  A  T  E  D  Z
B  V  I  L  M  A  D  E  M  G
D  L  G  C  I  G  L  U  L  R
X  I  C  Q  T  V  C  E  R  S
K  S  A  X  X  J  A  Y  K  V
N  T  R  X  H  I  L  L  D  B
O  E  E  X  Y  M  L  O  R  U
W  N  S  Y  M  A  E  V  T  U
S  S  W  N  B  E  D  E  F  K
Q  R  M  H  V  S  S  S  F  P
```

#65

```
X  K  F  D  W  W  N  N  J  J
T  S  O  P  R  O  M  I  S  E
Q  O  N  T  I  R  R  Q  B  I
S  Y  N  Q  T  D  P  R  I  X
Y  D  H  A  Y  T  S  P  B  P
P  H  O  R  B  N  T  R  O  L  Y
W  O  P  O  S  P  I  R  I  T  X
L  Y  E  V  N  Q  M  I  K  S  H
R  I  G  H  T  E  O  U  S  Q
```

#80

```
I  L  C  K  B  K  K  P  J  N
A  C  T  R  E  S  S  O  X  F
T  T  F  O  Z  I  M  L  W  A
S  V  H  B  F  U  D  I  E  M
F  I  L  L  D  A  S  T  A  O
A  U  J  N  M  E  C  M  L  U
H  E  S  Y  G  J  T  C  T  S
D  S  U  W  L  H  R  I  H  Q
T  S  K  C  X  P  B  N  Y  W
```

#90

```
A  W  I  O  O  S  Q  F  L  M
K  U  H  C  T  R  U  S  A  W
P  M  M  A  T  H  E  M  Y  T
J  R  H  M  T  Y  E  D  O  D
W  K  O  B  S  E  H  R  U  L
X  A  G  P  N  A  V  U  S  A
A  X  N  X  H  G  M  E  C  W
L  Q  M  T  O  E  M  E  R  L
S  T  Z  N  G  P  T  B  D  B
O  Y  U  W  Y  D  I  S  D  D
```

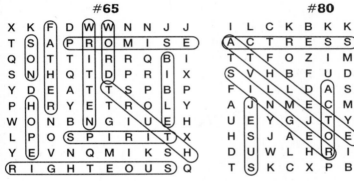
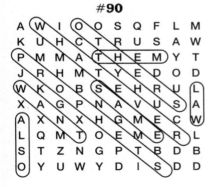

CODES

#10 — THE BIBLE IS GOD'S MESSAGE TO US

#25 — MY HELP COMES FROM THE LORD

#40 — CONDEMN and SAVE

#55 — GOD KNOWS OUR THOUGHTS

#70 — LEARNING HOW TO LIVE EACH DAY
IN A WAY PLEASING TO GOD

#85 — SAYING THINGS ABOUT A PERSON THAT
MAY NOT BE TRUE

#100 — GOD'S TRUTH NEVER CHANGES!

CROSSWORD PUZZLES

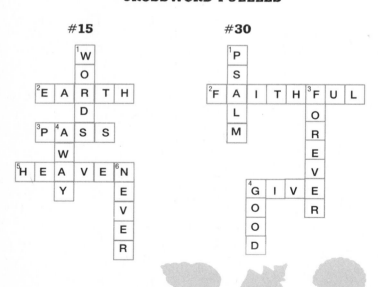

#15

#30

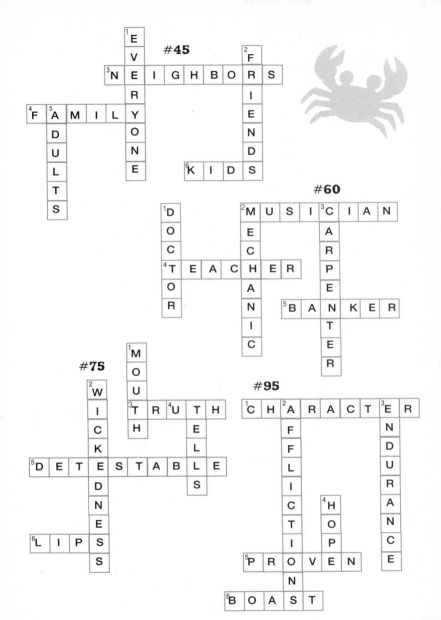

#45

Across:
3. NEIGHBORS
4. FAMILY
6. KIDS

Down:
1. EVERYONE
2. FRIEND
5. ADULTS

#60

Across:
2. MUSICIAN
4. TEACHER
5. BANKER

Down:
1. DOCTOR
2. MECHANIC
3. CARPENTER

#75

Across:
3. TRUTH
5. DETESTABLE
6. LIPS

Down:
1. MOUTH
2. WICKEDNESS
4. UELS

#95

Across:
1. CHARACTER
5. PROVEN
6. BOAST

Down:
2. AFFLICTION
3. ENDURANCE
4. HOPE